HERO DOGS

The author is donating all royalties from the sale of the first impression of this book, net of tax, to the Charity and 90% of subsequent impressions.

HERO DOGS

JANET MENZIES

In Aid of Hearing Dogs for Deaf People

Quiller

First published in the UK in 2012
by Quiller, an imprint of Quiller Publishing Ltd

British Library Cataloguing-in-Publication Data
A catalogue record for this book
is available from the British Library

ISBN 978 1 84689 143 4

Design and typesetting by Paul Saunders

Printed in China

Quiller

An imprint of Quiller Publishing Ltd

Wykey House, Wykey, Shrewsbury, SY4 1JA
Tel: 01939 261616 Fax: 01939 261606
E-mail: info@quillerbooks.com
Website: www.countrybooksdirect.com

For Tippy, who will always be remembered

CONTENTS

FOREWORD

DOGS ARE OUR FRIENDS and companions. They work hard to please us and give us boundless, unconditional love. They are also, as you will discover in reading this book, capable of acts of quiet heroism. I hope that these stories of heroic dogs will uplift you and move you, as they have me, and that you will find their deeds inspiring.

I have been a friend and supporter of Hearing Dogs for Deaf People for many years and the dogs trained by the charity give people with profound hearing problems invaluable independence, confidence and companionship. The money raised through the sale of this book will help train more dogs to undertake this important life-changing work so I would like to thank you for joining me in supporting these heroic hearing dogs and the people who train them.

BEN FOGLE

Supporter of Hearing Dogs for Deaf People

INTRODUCTION

BEATRICE FREDERIKA CLOUGH (always known as Babs) was born on 17 June 1910 in Connecticut USA. Her mother had been profoundly deaf for some years before Babs was born, having lost her hearing after a severe bout of malaria for which she was given huge doses of quinine.

Babs spent her early years living and travelling in Russia, China and Japan where her father was working. These days, travelling to remote corners of the globe would present very few problems and raise no eyebrows. But this profoundly deaf woman and her child would set out on their travels on whatever transport was available, rickshaws, buses, trains and tramp steamers without much idea of where they would end up, passing through places that rarely, if ever, saw foreigners. All through her childhood, Babs was her mother's sole 'carer' – acting as go-between in all interaction with the 'hearing' world and as her interpreter for all languages, including their own. Just as well that, by the time she was ten she could speak Russian, Japanese, Chinese and French. She never talked about the profound effect this must have had on her childhood but it is not hard to see where her determination to help deaf people found it's early inspiration.

Babs came to England to study at Oxford, married John Rathbone, a young Member of Parliament and they had two children. The war came, and after John Rathbone was killed while serving as a pilot in the RAF, she served as MP in his place (becoming the second American-born woman MP). In 1942 Babs married Paul Wright and gave birth to her daughter Faith, (the present Chairman of Hearing Dogs for Deaf People). After the retirement of her diplomat husband, Beatrice Wright finally had the opportunity to combine her determination to help deaf people and her love of dogs. She was also fascinated by the role that dogs could play in the lives of people with disabilities and realised that little, if anything, was being done to train dogs to help deaf people.

In 1980 Babs met Bruce Fogle, a Canadian veterinarian practising in London, at a scientific symposium (called The Human Companion Animal Bond) that Bruce had organised. Babs' Miniature Rough-haired Dachshund, Julia, gave her approval of Bruce and over the next

Faith Clark

Dr Bruce Fogle MBE

two years, the seeds of Hearing Dogs for Deaf People were sown. The Charity was launched at the world-famous Crufts dog show in 1982. Babs and Bruce separately visited two existing training centres in the United States and recruited an American trainer to visit the UK and share her experience with Hearing Dogs' first dog trainer, Tony Blunt (who went on to become the Charity's first Chief Executive). A veterinary colleague of Bruce's, Trevor Turner, provided grounds near Chinnor for a Portacabin that was used for training, and vital funding was provided by Pedigree Masterfoods, sufficient to cover half of the Charity's anticipated costs for the first three years.

Today, Hearing Dogs for Deaf People is a large national charity operating from two training centres; The Grange (the headquarters) in Buckinghamshire and the Beatrice Wright Centre in Yorkshire. Over the past thirty years, more than 1,600 life-changing partnerships between deaf people and hearing dogs have been created and there are around 750 working partnerships all over the UK being supported by the Charity. The Charity receives no government funding and is entirely dependent on public donations and legacies for income. It costs around £47,000 to train a hearing dog and support the resulting partnership for the working life of the hearing dog (approximately eight to ten years).

The Charity's research has identified that the most suitable breeds to train to become successful hearing dogs are typically Labradors, Golden Retrievers, Cocker Spaniels and Miniature Poodles (and crosses thereof). Some smaller breeds such as Cavalier King Charles Spaniels are also trained.

The Charity has its own Kennel Club Assured breeding scheme and works closely with a network of trusted breeders across the UK who generously donate suitable puppies for training. Very occasionally, puppies are also adopted from rescue centres as and when suitable recruits are identified.

The training of a hearing dog takes around eighteen to twenty-four months, consisting of initial puppy socialisation training with volunteers (eight weeks to twelve to fourteen months) before moving onto sound work training at one of our two training centres. Each applicant is individually matched with a dog and the training reflects their specific individual needs. The deaf person and hearing dog then spend a period of time training together at home before qualifying as an official partnership. Hearing dogs are registered assistance dogs and wear a distinctive burgundy coat to identify them and permit them access when out and about.

Hearing dogs alert their deaf partners to household sounds and danger alerts in the home, at work and in public places by touching them with a paw or nudging with a nose to gain attention. But the sound work is only part of the role a hearing dog plays in the life of its deaf partner.

Deafness can be a devastating, invisible disability and often leaves people feeling desperately lonely and isolated. A hearing dog not only provides a deaf person with the confidence to lead an independent life, but is a loving companion giving unconditional love and acceptance.

FAITH CLARK, Chairman of Trustees, and

DR BRUCE FOGLE MBE, Co-founder of Hearing Dogs for Deaf People

PUPPIES, FRIENDS AND SUPPORTERS

A litter ready to start basic training

All this training can be tiring!

Although parents take charge of the training, it's fun for all the family

Tim Vincent has been a long-term supporter of Hearing Dogs

EastEnders actress Rita Simons with hearing dog puppy Jasper

Puppies specially bred for Hearing Dogs

Even snow won't deter a hearing dog!

Hearing Dogs for Deaf People's 'poster pup' for puppy sponsorship

ACKNOWLEDGEMENTS

THIS BOOK IS ABOUT the heroic achievements of dogs, but of course every dog comes along with its own human colleague – and in some cases there is a whole organisation backing up the dog's work. We dog lovers are often accused of being overly sentimental about our dogs, and this may be true, but it is undeniable that through working together, the people and dogs in this book have contributed to making the world a better place. So with my sincerest gratitude for their tremendous dedication and commitment, thank you to these organisations and individuals.

Hearing Dogs For Deaf People, with special thanks to the executive and media team. The 1st Military Working Dog Regiment. The People's Dispensary for Sick Animals (PDSA) who award the Dickin and Gold Medals for animal bravery. The Search And Rescue Dog Association (SARDA), especially SARDA England, SARDA Wales, SARDA Ireland North and SARDA Lakes. The Kennel Club, whose Charitable Trust helps many of the organisations in this book, and who give Friends for Life awards annually at Crufts. Kent Police Dog Unit. Mike Dewar of the Greater Manchester Fire Service. The UK Border Agency. Medical Detection Dogs, the joint organisation of Cancer + Bio-detection Dogs and Medical Alert Dogs. Support Dogs UK. Canine Partners. Dogs for the Disabled. Dog AID. The Animals in War Memorial Trust. More details on how to give to these organisations or get involved can be found at the back of the book.

Many individuals provided huge amounts of personal support and time in the research for this book, especially: Simon Anderson; Michelle Bell; Tony Brown-Griffin; Maureen Burns; Sir Edward Dashwood; Joanne Day; Anne Heading; Lou Holmes; His Grace the Duke of Northumberland; Keith Reynolds (cartoonist creator of 'Dog'); Collin Singer of Wagtail UK; Alan Stewart, of Cairngorm Sleddog Centre; Ann Ramsden; Glen Tallett.

The black and white cartoons appear courtesy of The Cartoon Bank: p. 37 © Leo Cullum/The New Yorker Collection; p. 57 © Arnie Levin/The New Yorker Collection; p. 59 © Danny Shanahan/The New Yorker Collection; p. 95 © Peter Steiner/The New Yorker Collection.

CHAPTER ONE

BEST FRIENDS IN BURGUNDY COATS

Hearing Dogs for Deaf People at Work

ASURPRISING THING happened not long after Jason Bell's new hearing dog, Violet, arrived at the family home in East Yorkshire. Jason's mother, Michelle, started hearing laughter. Jason was nine when he received her, and Violet, a black Labrador cross Retriever, was only eighteen months old herself. The Bell family had been selected as one of the first to pilot a ground-breaking programme by Hearing Dogs for Deaf People to place 'team' dogs with profoundly deaf children, normally considered too young for the responsibility of looking after a dog – hence the phrase 'team' as the whole family would be involved. Jason's mother, Michelle, takes up the story: 'It was shortly after we'd got Violet, I could hear laughter and giggling coming from upstairs. So I went up to Jason's room, and he and Violet were there playing together, and she was jumping around, and they were having a lovely time. It was strange because it was so different. I realised then that we had been missing that.'

Jason told his Mum: 'I'm happy now, I was very sad and lonely before, but now I've got Violet, she's my best friend.' And Violet's arrival

transformed family life at the Bells' home from then onwards. Michelle says: 'The laughter we have now. I can't remember a time when we didn't have her. It is like we've always had her. To see Jason with her is wonderful, there is a bond and a friendship between them. She is there all the time for him – it is an unconditional love.'

Hearing dog Violet with Jason Bell

But it was also hard for the family to realise just how lonely Jason's profound deafness had made him feel, because Jason had been making the best of things. Michelle remembers: 'He'd never said he was lonely. He was always a happy boy on the outside – but a bit shy and found it hard to get involved with what was going on around him.' So the family knew they needed to do something to give Jason ways of finding companionship. 'Jason was lonely outside of school,' explains his mum: 'He has friends at his school for deaf children, but all the children live so far away from the school. We tried sleep-overs and so on, but there is only so much you can do as a parent. Jason never complained or said he was lonely, but I knew he must be. We'd reached the point of looking for a rescue dog for him to have. Then the head of Jason's unit showed us a flyer from Hearing Dogs for Deaf People about a pilot scheme they were launching to place hearing dogs with very young deaf children. I was straight on the phone about it, and we were accepted for a place on the scheme.'

Little did Michelle know just how much life was going to change! First of all, a suitable young dog had to be found for the family. Violet was perfect – especially as she has her own slight disability. She is partially blind in one eye, which meant that although she had been bred as a Guide Dog for the Blind, that career path was no longer open. The partially-sighted leading the blind isn't recommended! But Violet had literally been born to serve, with a wonderful temperament and the ability to learn and communicate. So Jan Smith and her colleagues at the Hearing Dogs 'team' dog project knew that she would be an ideal candidate for training.

Violet moved into a smart kennels at Hearing Dogs' headquarters at The Grange, Saunderton, near Princes Risborough in Buckinghamshire. Using rewards like her favourite toys and occasional food treats (very welcome for a Labrador cross!) Violet's natural behaviours were educated so that she could use them to communicate with a deaf child. As a retriever breed it was instinctive for Violet to want to carry objects in her mouth and bring them back to people when asked. So a small purse was made in which Violet could carry notes to and from people. The mother of a deaf child can't simply shout down the garden path when she wants her little boy to come in for tea – but Violet would be able to carry a note from her, saying: 'Stop playing and come in … or else!'

Even more necessary would be teaching Violet to alert a deaf person to important sounds: smoke or fire alarms, the door bell or telephone, wake-up calls – all the many sounds we all rely on every day without noticing it until we can't hear them. Violet was trained that when she heard the alarm clock go off in the morning, she would go to Jason and nudge him with her nose to wake him up. Like all hearing dogs,

Violet does, of course, come with a snooze facility! If Jason doesn't feel like getting up immediately, she will let him have a few more minutes before using both paws to deliver a rather firmer push on the sleepy-head's arm. It can be very amusing for families to watch the thorough blitzing that follows for a real lazy-bones. Michelle Bell says: 'That alone makes life easier. Before, I would have to go in to Jason about ten times in the morning. But now Violet wakes him up for school, and he gets up straight away to go down and feed her.'

That's convenient enough, but the potentially life-saving skill that Violet has learnt is to alert Jason to the sound of other, more serious, alarms. This is especially important at night. Many parents of deaf children report that their child is understandably scared of being alone in bed unable to hear anything that may be happening. Their children don't sleep well, or have nightmares, and usually have to sleep with the door open and a light on, or very often end up back in the parents' bedroom even as they are growing up. But once Violet started sleeping in Jason's room he no longer felt the need to have a light on or leave the door open. Violet's training showed her how to alert Jason to sounds by nudging him gently with her nose, then leading him to the source of the sound. For danger signals she will nudge and then drop to the floor to indicate that there is a risk.

With Violet's basic training complete, it was time for her to meet the Bells so that she and the family could learn to work together. This bonding and mutual training process is very important if a partnership is to work long-term, so Hearing Dogs for Deaf People has specialist facilities, both at the Saunderton headquarters, and at the northern centre at Bielby in North Yorkshire. There are charming little cottages where the family or individual hearing dog recipient will live for a week alongside their new dog. The cottages can be adapted so that they are as similar to the recipients' homes as possible. If the recipient's home has a particular lay-out they need their dog to become accustomed to, then this can be replicated, along with front doorbells, oven timers etc.

Michelle remembers: 'We went to meet Violet and it went really well straight away. And then the time came when we all went to stay at the centre to get trained with her and from day one Jason and Violet worked really well together.'

The trainers at Hearing Dogs had certain goals that they wanted to achieve in the pilot project. Jan explains: 'Like all hearing dogs we taught Violet to alert to sounds whether alarm clocks or fire alarms or general dangers. And we also taught her to go to Jason either to bring him back to his mother or deliver a message Violet carries in a small purse carried in her mouth. This is similar to the things a hearing dog does for an adult recipient. But in addition we had the idea that the dog would walk on a "join-up" lead. This means that the "team" leader – Jason's mum Michelle in this case – has Violet walking in a harness with two leads. She holds one and Jason holds the other lead attached to Violet's collar. We hoped that this would give Jason pride in walking his dog but also "anchor" him, to avoid him running off into possible danger where Michelle wouldn't be able to call him.'

This objective succeeded even more than the trainers had hoped. Michelle confesses: 'When he was about five, before we got Violet, Jason was a wanderer! One minute he was there and the next he was gone, and you couldn't see him. I have been frantic in Morrisons before now looking for him – because they can't put anything over the tannoy, both for child protection and because he wouldn't be able to hear it. Once we were searching everywhere, even the toilets, and we couldn't find him.'

When Jason reappeared it turned out he'd been using the disabled toilet – logical to him, but the one place his frantic mum hadn't searched! 'Now Violet is there,' says Michelle, 'and when we first got her, that dual lead was a godsend. But as Jason has got older he now has the dog on his own. Jason is growing up, and they are growing up together. We do a lot of camping and we have a caravan with an awning for the children. Jason had always wanted to sleep under the awning, and now he's old enough, with Violet there we feel safe to let him. Violet is part of the family. It has just become an everyday thing for us all. We use "the call" all the time to go and get him for things, but you just don't think about it.

'For example, if he's out in the garden on the trampoline, we'll send Violet down with a note for him. She has taught herself to jump onto the trampoline and lie flat, which deadens the bounce and brings Jason to a halt! Then he can read the note and usually sends me one back via Violet-mail. She can even swim into the sea to fetch him back. We used to have to be with Jason all the time, but Violet's taken over that role – she even keeps the whole family all rounded up together, which is really handy for me!'

So Violet has certainly met every expectation set for her by her trainers – but she's done more than that, and helped Jason in ways that they and the family never expected. Michelle tries to put her finger on that indefinable extra something: 'Having Violet has given Jason confidence and independence. He's thirteen now and Violet has been the one there for him, to help him grow up. Before we had Violet, people didn't know how to react to Jason – and I have been surprised at the amount of people who have been really rude to him. They never saw his deafness before, it was invisible. But now Violet's alongside him in her burgundy Hearing Dogs jacket – and she wears her Blue Peter badge, which has become a great conversation starter.

Having Violet has given Jason confidence and independence

'The other day we were in Caffè Nero and I sent Jason to bag us a table upstairs while I was queuing. As I went up the stairs, I could see there was a lady and she and Jason were having a chat. So I went to explain, and she stopped me and said, "It's OK, we know all about it, and your boy's dog is three and half years old and he's told us she's called Violet …" And I was thinking, "oh, OK" because that hadn't happened before, and it was strange, but really nice.'

Recently Violet was even outperforming her Guide Dog cousins: 'We were having breakfast at the supermarket and Violet as usual was just sitting quietly under the table and this Guide Dog came in with his family and it has to be said he was making a real nuisance of himself and getting under everybody's feet – it was awful! Then we got up to go and Violet came out from under the table, and everybody said, "Oh she's so quiet we didn't even know she was there," and of course the Bell family was bursting with pride!'

But Violet isn't always a paragon of virtue. When she is off duty she jumps around playing and lets off steam. 'She can be a bit naughty occasionally,' admits Michelle, 'The other day she stole some chocolate. When I came back she looked so guilty and I discovered she had had a big chocolate bar. She is a lovely natured dog – but she is very protective of Jason. She is quite assertive, if for example a stranger comes up to the car. "I am looking after him," is her attitude. She isn't at all happy if she ever thinks people might hurt Jason.' Ready as she is, luckily Violet never has had to step in and save Jason – but in a sense she has already done much more than that. Thanks to Violet joining the family, Jason has turned thirteen as a happy and confident boy, looking forward to enjoying being a teenager to the full, with all that entails!

Ann Ramsden's hearing dog experience is at the opposite end of the spectrum from Jason's, because Ann grew up with normal hearing, and began to lose it almost too imperceptibly to notice: 'It happened very gradually,' remembers Ann. 'I had always had sinus and ENT problems since I was a child but they didn't bother me overly. I was in the forces, in the Military Police, and then the infections got worse and I had more operations and it just crept up on me and I couldn't hear the phone and I couldn't hear my colleagues at work. You want to try to pretend and fit in as you always have. It is difficult to get your mind round not being A1 fitness any more. Reclassifying yourself is not easy.'

Without much of a support network, and in many ways unwilling to acknowledge even to herself that she now needed some help, Ann began to feel isolated. 'I'm divorced, with a daughter, and as she grew up I realised I could hear her less and less, until I couldn't really hear her any more. I couldn't hear if she called me in the night and I used to sleep really badly. It was so hard for me to relax – especially with it being only her and me.' Having hearing aids fitted certainly enabled Ann to

*Hearing dog Max with
Ann Ramsden*

hear while she was wearing them, but they couldn't help when she took
them out to go to sleep at night, nor could they take the place of friends
and social life. But Ann read about Hearing Dogs for Deaf People: 'I saw
an advert asking for volunteers to become socialisers for hearing dog
puppies before they went into training.' It was a disappointment for Ann
to discover that she lived too far from the training centre for it to be
practical for her to socialise a pup, but all the same she maintained her
interest in the Charity. 'Then I got a letter from an organiser saying they
wanted to start a branch locally to me and would I like to come along
to a meeting to plan it. There was quite a big crowd at the meeting, with
two or three hearing dogs. I cried at that meeting. I was so moved to see

the difference that having a hearing dog was making to their owners. And also, it was the first time I had ever gone anywhere where I felt like I could be a deaf person – and it felt like coming home.'

But emotions were very mixed for Ann. After her initial disappointment over not becoming a puppy socialiser, an additional worry for her was that she felt that, with the improved hearing given her by her aids, she wouldn't qualify to become a hearing dog recipient. Ironically, she feared she just wasn't deaf enough. She stuck with her involvement with the Charity though, and entered a happy phase in her life as she became secretary of the newly formed branch. 'It is such an uplifting environment at the Charity's headquarters at The Grange near Saunderton. I remember I used to drive down the M40 and I couldn't wait to get there – I would be singing at the top of my voice as I bombed along the motorway, heaven knows what it sounded like.'

Despite her misgivings, Ann applied for a dog, and with her application processed, waited for her audiology report. 'My report came through, and basically it said I was not deaf enough. That was awful.' Even now there's a choke in Ann's voice as she remembers that horrible time when her worst fears were realised. She was suffering all the stress, loneliness and anxiety of the condition, but sadly those factors don't register on the scientific scale. 'I was down to go for another hearing test a few months later,' Ann remembers, 'and in just that time my hearing had really deteriorated.' Ann finally qualified for a dog, and after an eighteen-month wait, was offered a three-year-old Poodle cross. 'I met her and she was a dream.' Like the Bells, Ann did her pre-placement week at The Grange, Saunderton, and all went well. But yet another disappointment was to follow. When an excited Ann finally brought her new hearing dog back home, she discovered it was not cat-compatible: 'It was on the Friday night, I discovered she had a real thing about cats. She wasn't good at all with my cat, so one of the trainers had to come and take her back to The Grange.'

It seemed Ann's rocky road had taken another downward dive. 'I went to The Grange, where there were three dogs waiting to be matched with the right deaf recipient. One of them was a Japanese Chin, and I am quite a big, sporty woman and really, it just wasn't for me. As for the second dog, which was a Papillon, I'm sure it was sweet – but to me it looked like breakfast on a lid!' Surely Ann's dream of having a hearing dog wasn't finally going to disappear after all she had been through? 'Then they brought out a young yellow Labrador, and it was Max. Instantly we adored each other.' Instinctively Ann knew this was it. A new happy chapter in her life was about to begin.

'Max had come to Hearing Dogs from a family who couldn't keep him. He was a youngster and hadn't finished his training. He was good with the cats and went through his sound work training and we had our pre-placement week and it all went so well. And so Max came home. The sense of relief of having Max is simply not describable. It was like a physical feeling of taking off this heavy winter coat and the stress drained away from me overnight. It had been a thick blanket of anxiety and depression that I hadn't even realised was there until it went. It was an actual physical feeling of it being lifted off me. I felt as if I was protected and loved. When you are on your own and you are a deaf person it is hard to make relationships. Social interactions are difficult. Your confidence is low and you don't want to talk to people.

'That's all changed since Max has joined me. He has broadened my social circle. And he paves the way for me to meet people. He is so handsome and he has his Hearing Dogs burgundy coat on, which is a great ice-breaker. The assumption is that a deaf person signs, but as someone who has gradually become deaf, I don't sign very much. But now teenagers will come up and try signing, and we all practise together, which can be very funny.'

Ann now works full time for Hearing Dogs for Deaf People and has recently moved up to Yorkshire to be based at the new Beatrice Wright Centre at Bielby. It is clear as she chats that Max has transformed her life in more ways than even she dreamed of during those years when she so desperately wanted a hearing dog. Obviously Max is a professional who performs all the sound alerts, message-carrying etc. that he has been trained to do, but there is clearly more to it than that. Max brings his own initiative and personality to bear on his relationship with Ann.

She explains: 'Max is a dream. He is funny, he is serious, he is caring. He works like a trooper. Nothing stops him from working.

'He is extremely fond of children. One day we were at a demonstration event and he was entertaining a whole group of children. Basically he was this dog just buried under a pile of children all playing with him. Then suddenly the fire alarm went and it was like a dog coming out of water and shaking himself. Max rose up from out of this pile of children and shook them off like water, so he could come to me and give me the alert.

'He very much loves his cuddles, but he is very determined about his work. He is called Mister Cool at the office. He won't be distracted by anything if he thinks I need to be told something. I remember not long after I came to work for Hearing Dogs, the fire alarm test went off. Max was lying under the desk as usual. He jumped up so quickly to alert me for the alarm that he actually cracked his head on the desk – but he still staggered over to alert me! He never misses anything. He wakes me up to the alarm clock and does it gently but persistently, and he gives me a smile and seems to have a wink in his eye. The girl I work with here in the office said she is jealous of me and Max because she knows we have had a conversation but she doesn't know what we have said. She's right, but we don't talk politics – it is either love or food with him! He's eight now and I do have to watch his weight. However one of his most consistent alerts that he gives me is still for lunch and coffee breaks!'

As deaf people talk about their hearing dogs, it becomes very clear that these animals are not furry robots, but genuine companions with their own personalities, and sometimes their own agenda! They work as equals alongside their deaf human, with both partners doing the thinking, and only one having the ears. A good temperament is obviously vital for a working dog, especially one that will be in public, and so all the hearing dogs are loving and gentle. But their deaf recipients often comment on other characteristics that cannot be trained for, but are equally important. The dogs have to be confident in themselves, and be able to take the initiative where necessary. 'Determined, professional, wise, thoughtful' are all words deaf people use to describe their dogs to try to express the fact that although trained to do a job, their dogs bring their own personal take to the relationship.

This has been a particularly good experience for Glen Tallett from Kent, who is both profoundly deaf and wheelchair-bound through cerebral palsy. Glen received a hearing dog, Milly, in 1999, who became his inseparable partner. But Glen was surprised to discover that in addition to the normal hearing dog alerts that she was trained for, Milly worked out that because of being in a wheelchair he would need further assistance. So Milly taught herself to pick up items for Glen. The years went by, and the time inevitably came for Milly to retire. But seeing what Milly had achieved gave Glen the idea that perhaps it would be possible for his next dog to be specifically trained to help with the full range of his disabilities – in other words to be a dual-purpose dog. Glen was right. By 2009 he was in partnership with Geri, one of the country's first ever dual assistance dogs.

Glen tells how it all came to be: 'Before she retired, Milly and I went to an event where we saw Andy Cook from Canine Partners. I've known Andy for ten years as he was involved with Milly's training for me at Hearing Dogs. With Andy was Geri, a young chocolate Labrador, and

Hearing dog Geri with Glen Tallett

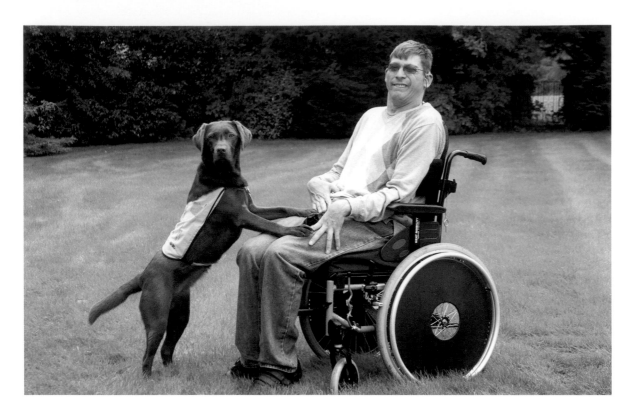

Glen worked very hard with Geri, and this shows in the close bond they developed

Andy showed me how Geri knew some tasks already. I loved her from the first time I saw her. Andy said he was sure Geri could learn all the task work and sound work, and it would be the first time that Canine Partners and Hearing Dogs would work together.' The two charities worked out a schedule for Geri to learn both the sound work and all the tasks she needed to perform to help Glen. Vicky, from Canine Partners, trained Geri to perform all her task work and remembers Geri's personality: 'Geri was a very lovely sweet and gentle dog and was a pleasure to train. Glen had a long list of tasks that he required. Fortunately Geri was a quick learner and loved it all. It was also important for me to adapt my training and stop using verbal commands as Glen doesn't have speech.'

After the task work training, Geri moved to the Hearing Dogs training centre, where Nikki Hawkes undertook training her to respond to everyday sounds. Nikki says: 'Geri was very bright and picked things up quickly. I had to learn how to train a dog for a wheelchair user, and keep using the Canine Partner commands so that her training was consistent. Her favourite sound was the alarm clock, and she worked reliably for this all through her training, as I can testify as I took her home each night! Glen worked very hard with Geri, and this showed in the close bond they developed.'

Although Milly was elderly, she stayed with Glen, and she and Geri got on very well. In March 2009, Geri became Glen's dual-purpose assistance dog, and with much support from both Canine Partners and Hearing Dogs she took to her role extremely well. Glen uses a mobility scooter to get around outside, and Geri would walk alongside the scooter with Milly riding on the platform. When Milly eventually died of old age, it was Geri who comforted her boss. 'I'm so glad I had Geri to help when Milly passed away,' says Glen. On a daily basis Geri performed an amazing range of tasks with Glen, enabling him to have an independence that would be impossible without her. Glen lists: 'Geri pulled off my shoes, socks and jeans. She fetched things for me, opened and closed doors. And she learnt to pick up boxes, cans and other things from my kitchen cupboards and supermarket shelves. She started taking paper from my printer and giving it to me, something she did herself – I did not teach her. She was very clever and learnt my needs without me having to tell her. She was very quick to respond to the doorbell, telephone, cooker timer, mobile phone, alarm clock and smoke alarm. The only difficulty she had to begin with was opening the washing machine door as she has quite a small mouth and the handle is hard. Howerver, we found a way round it and she became very good at it. Geri also learned my signal for when I need help and she could push the Lifeline button. Geri and I became very close friends and partners.' Unfortunately Geri had to be retired early from her dual-purpose role. Glen misses her enormously while he awaits her successor. 'Geri was clever and sometimes very funny,' remembers Glen. 'If she was bored and there were no sounds for her to alert to or no tasks that I needed, she would go to the hall and switch the lights on with her nose! She always licked my ear, which tickled. I taught Geri new tasks, and even to do a High Five when she had been a good girl.'

But no matter how many day-to-day jobs round the house a dog takes on board, what their recipients value most is the dog's freely given friendship. This was especially important for a nine-year-old severely deaf child, Evie, and her hearing 'team' dog, Gem, a yellow Labrador. Evie received Gem in 2008, and her parents Dave and Becky knew that Gem was the answer right from the moment they went to The Grange for their partnership training – that night it was the first night in her

Hearing dog Gem with Evie and her mother Becky © *Sheffield Star*

whole life that Evie slept in her own room on her own. She wanted to do it because she felt safer with Gem. Evie's mum, Becky remembers: 'Before we had Gem, Evie had never, not even once, slept through the night in her own bed. So the most exciting event is Evie sleeping in her own bed. Now she goes to bed at 7.30pm and gets up the next morning at 7.00am. After seven-and-a-half years' broken sleep and sometimes quite upsetting and traumatic nights it is fantastic for us as her parents, but I can only imagine how immensely more secure Evie must be feeling if she is now able to sleep like this.'

For deaf children growing up, one of the most difficult things to come to terms with is that their freedom has to be slightly curtailed – not because they are not old enough, simply because they can't hear well. To an intelligent child wanting to grow up and test boundaries, this must be

Evie and her hearing 'team' dog, Gem, a yellow Labrador

really frustrating. Evie's parents certainly felt that this must be difficult for her. Becky explains: 'She's very intelligent and attempts to be more independent than she is capable of being, which leads to frustration. She could resort to being quite naughty when she felt she was being ignored. However, both Dave and I have noticed a dramatic improvement since Gem's arrival.

'We think this is because with Gem, Evie never feels ignored and Evie knows that she must do as Gem is telling her with the nose nudge alert. She seems not to need as much attention now Gem is here.' Recently Evie told her mum: 'I don't get into any trouble now Gem is here.' Another big plus for Evie is that she is no longer shattered from her sleepless nights. Evie's schoolwork has benefited massively from her improved rest. And like many of the 'team' children, she is much less shy than she used to be. Becky says: 'She had always been the quiet one at school, but the school had a session specially for Evie to tell the other pupils and teachers all about Gem and we were amazed when she stood at the front of the class, and spoke non-stop for a full five minutes. This was incredible for us, another fantastic breakthrough. The talk that Evie gave led to a question and answer session with the children about Evie's deafness, which she has never done before. When she came home from school she was smiling when she told us, you could hear the pride in her voice. This was a truly touching moment for us.'

This new-found confidence goes beyond the classroom. Becky explains: 'We went on a shopping trip recently and a lady asked Evie about Gem and asked if she could stroke her. Evie explained that she could, but only on Gem's shoulders as she wasn't allowed too much fuss when she was working. In the past, Evie would have clutched hold of my leg and looked the other way if an adult tried to talk to her. A good level of social interaction is important to us as her parents. Evie is who she is, we don't want her to hide behind her hearing aids, we want her to be proud of everything she is and to know that deafness is just a tiny little part of her. We believe that because of the pride she feels in having Gem she now wants to share her feelings and experiences with anyone who asks her.'

Like so many 'team' dog families, Becky finds all Gem's trained alerts helpful in a practical way, but what has really transformed the family's life is Gem's role as a family member. She echoes Michelle in saying: 'It feels like Gem has lived with us for much longer than she has. And with Evie it's like we have a child who is beginning to blossom. It is so heartening that Gem's had such a positive impact on our lives. The other day Evie and Gem were laid on the lounge rug together, both totally shattered after a lovely walk, and I listened without Evie knowing as she whispered to Gem how much she loved her. That about says it all really, doesn't it?'

"I know you're a working dog, Angus.
I just don't have anything for you right now."

FAMOUS FACES...

Supporting Hearing Dogs for Deaf People

Camilla and Kevin Sacre-Dallerup are supporters of Hearing Dogs

Rula Lenska demonstrates that hearing dogs come in all shapes and sizes

Kate Humble has been a long-term Hearing Dogs supporter

Matt Baker has been a supporter of Hearing Dogs since he donated a puppy in 2005

As a hearing impaired actress, Stephanie Beacham enjoys her links with Hearing Dogs

Former world heavyweight boxing champion, Frank Bruno at a recent Hearing Dogs event

left Keen supporters Erin Boag and Anton du Beke with a hearing dog puppy

39

CHAPTER TWO

THE FIRE IN THE DOG

*Civilian Dogs Working in the
Emergency Services*

The saying goes: 'Cometh the hour, cometh the man,' but when it comes to Mike Dewar of the Greater Manchester Fire Service and his dog Echo, it is more a case of: 'Come a disaster, here comes the dog.' The call for Echo goes out all the time, but the toughest emergency he ever answered came on 14 January 2010, when he and Mike arrived in Haiti to help with the search for victims of the devastating earthquake. Mike remembers the moment very well: 'It was below freezing in Manchester, and Echo's kennel is outside. We got off the plane in Haiti and it was over 100 degrees Fahrenheit, so adapting to the heat was the first problem to overcome.

'On that very first day, we did eight searches, and Echo was having to walk over bodies to look for the living. In England we wouldn't do more than two searches a day, but in Haiti we were doing ten searches a day. We searched a school one day and there were 100 children, all dead. Every house was awful. It was too hot, we had to drive Echo round in a United Nations vehicle because it had air conditioning. We searched

Greater Manchester Fire Service search dog Echo working in debris

a building and it was like sticking your head in an oven. Echo got heat exhaustion at one point. The thing is, he would not stop searching. He is very focused when he is on search, he has this incredible drive. If there is somebody there he will find them. In Haiti he went on until he collapsed and had to be put on a drip. Even in the rest period it was hard for him because we were camping, and working dogs need a quiet place for their down time. I remember we built a bath of cold water for him to sit in, and he would lie down in the bath with just his nose poking up!

'The Caribbean market search was terrible for both of us. Echo was coming back from searches with body fluids all over him. He was very quiet after that. It took it out of him. It was just so many negative searches, and Echo needed a positive outcome for his morale, so we hid a live person in the rubble so he could find him. That made a difference, Echo perked back up again. I have spoken to an animal psychologist since then, and he said dogs can get depressed. I don't think ultimately you can really train any dog for an experience as extreme as Haiti.'

Echo after the Haiti Earthquake © *Sun Features*

Yet Echo was destined to be a search dog from birth. His father was a cave rescue dog and his mother a drug detection dog. Greater Manchester Fire and Rescue Service has for many years had a search and rescue team which regularly travels abroad to help in emergencies and disasters. In the aftermath of 9/11 it was decided that the team would be much more effective with a canine capability. Mike remembers: 'I had seen search dogs working in America and India and been very impressed, so I went and bought a dog off my own bat – Echo was the first dog I had ever owned in my life!'

But it seems as though Echo knew this was the right thing, because Mike is convinced: 'Echo picked us. We saw an advert about working Lab puppies for sale, and the family and I went to look and we had almost decided on buying a different pup from the litter. But then this little yellow one came up to me and when I went to put him down again he wouldn't let go. We all realised he was the one.'

Even though he was only just over three months old, Echo's basic training started as soon as the Dewar family got him home. There was just one problem: 'With him being our first dog, we didn't really know how to train him! But we learned off the internet and we got advice from people. And it helped that Echo could basically do it anyway – it was in him. Any problems were down to our lack of knowledge. I remember we had Echo in the house at first. Then I went to America on a course and when I got back he had wrecked the place! I said, "Where's the dog?" and he was in a kennel outside!

'The first thing with training was to get him barking when he made a find, that's a basic. With my second dog I made the mistake of leaving it six months. The training is really play for the dogs, they are mad for it. But you need to have a dog with an inbuilt drive to seek and play. The experts said you will soon know if it's there. And they were right – straight away Echo was bombed out on his toys and he would do anything for this toy, searching for it and finding it and barking. We trained him on squeaky toys. Echo is eight now, an old man – but if he hears a squeak in the street or wherever he will go mad for it!

'So I was doing the training, but I didn't know how to progress to searching for people. But – I can't work out how – Echo seemed to get the idea anyway and twelve months down the line he instinctively knew what to do. My son, Daniel, was hiding in ditches for Echo to find him and actually got an award for it. But he did hide in a lot of ditches! Echo is very headstrong and searches in his own way but he will always find. I trust him 100 per cent and I have come to respect his dominant side. That is his personality. You need a dog like that to be able to search in somewhere like Haiti where it is such high stress. You don't want them to be bothered about it.'

Echo eventually qualified as a search dog in 2006, and almost immediately his first job took him to the site of a collapsed mill building in Lancaster, where conditions were very different from training. 'In training you set things up for the dog to be successful,' explains Mike, 'but here there was this huge rubble pile and it was full of pigeons and very tricky. On a rubble pile Echo works about ten feet from me but he can work up to 400 feet away on open ground. I don't direct him at all.'

Since that first search, Echo has helped pioneer all sorts of new techniques. Mike explains: 'We have a harness that we can lower him in, similar to that used by a mountaineer, but you have to be careful because

Echo with Mike Dewar on a rubble pile

it is a snag hazard. He goes up in the helicopter quite a bit and can either jump out if it is near enough to the ground or be winched down, with me following after him. With the fire engines we go up in the cage and I hook him up – I remember once I carried him up a ladder forty feet in the air and he panicked. I thought "if you are going, I am going too" and just at that moment a fireman managed to grab us both back onto the ladder.'

These days Echo is a famous dog and he and Mike do a lot of community work, including open days and talks at schools. But he doesn't let his celebrity status get in the way of the job. Mike says: 'If he is onto a find he is like a monomaniac, he is transfixed. Off duty he has the softest nature, but then he puts his protective boots on and that tells him it's time to go to work.' When Echo got back from Haiti he had to go into quarantine for six months, a poor reward for his heroic service. But since then, says Mike: 'He has been given so many honours. We went to Crufts for an award nomination, and we were there with all the assistance dogs, and they were so steady and calm – and then there was Echo! But they say it's not the dog in the fire, it is the fire in the dog.'

Since his success with Echo, Mike has added several more dogs to the team, including training a specialist fire investigation dog, Cracker (known at home as Lucy), who, aged only five, has rapidly become an ace detective. Mike says: 'Her official role is forensic crime scene investigation, where she concentrates on detecting accelerants used to set a fire, basically it is CSI Miami but with dogs. She gets 400 calls a year and so far has had more than 100 successful finds. We had a typical example recently of a guy who had set a fire, but got home and had washed and changed his clothes – but not his baseball cap. This guy was cocky, he'd put his cap back on. Cracker got the scent off his cap straight away. When I search a suspect I say, tell me now, because the dog will find it. People are beginning to believe me – there is a new sheriff in town, and her name is Cracker!'

Echo at the Friends for Life Awards © *The Kennel Club, Friends for Life*

Despite his confidence in her, even Mike is surprised sometimes by the extent of Cracker's detection abilities. 'A guy had poured petrol through someone's letter box to set the fire. He'd had the petrol in a Budweiser beer bottle and when he got home he threw the empty bottle out into his garden, which was completely littered with empty Budweiser bottles. There must have been 200 old bottles in the back yard and Cracker found the one bottle among them that had had the petrol in it. The offender's prints were on the bottle and Cracker's evidence got him convicted. Another time, the offender had set fire to the home and emptied the accelerant container down the sink. Cracker jumped up in the sink, she was going mad scrabbling at the plug hole, but none of us could smell anything until we opened up the u-bend and found traces of the accelerant.'

At the Kent Police Dog Unit, officers are equally impressed with the achievements of their own canine constabulary, not just in the field of forensic investigation, but throughout police work. PC Neil Loudon explained: 'We have thirty general purpose dogs, mostly German Shepherds and Belgian Malinois, and they can track, search for property, search for offenders and missing people and help keep public order. But in addition we have a number of specialist dogs like my dog, Snoop, whose main job is to sniff out drugs. Snoop was a stray who came to us from Battersea Dogs Home. He is a working Cocker Spaniel (a gundog breed), crossed with another gundog breed, a Retriever – plus something else, but we're not quite sure what! He has a very high drive to work and search, and when he was first rescued was a bit naughty, so Battersea were finding it a bit difficult to re-home him.'

But police work proved to be the making of Snoop, and his affectionate bond with PC Loudon is obvious. 'We had a drugs call out only this morning where Snoop found some cannabis,' said PC Loudon, 'It was a difficult job for him because it was on a farm and he had to cope with the very strong smell of the pigs, but he managed to do that. Our dogs usually retire when they are eight or nine years old, so over the years they do get very experienced. The shift can be eight hours or ten hours. I will work him for twenty to twenty-five minutes and then he has a rest,

Search training in progress

especially for his nose! You want to avoid the dog getting nasal fatigue, as well as getting physically tired. He chills out in his special car kennel.'

Sniffer dogs like Snoop conduct two main types of search. A passive search most of us will have noticed at airports where the dog simply sits and sniffs as people are walking past. Labradors are especially good at the patient sitting required for this! In an active search, the dogs go into buildings and vehicles on a specific quest. This suits Cocker Spaniels like Snoop, not just because of their more restless natures, but their smaller size means they can get into all the little hiding places. PC Loudon told me what he and Snoop do on a search: 'In phase one, we go into the room and Snoop goes where he wants, and very often that will be a result. But if he doesn't cover the room fully, for example going into small spaces or under furniture, then I can direct him into those areas, so it is a team effort. But you have to be careful not to influence the dog, because that could affect any court proceedings later.'

There's no doubt that Snoop and his canine colleagues get a lot of job satisfaction from their work. PC Loudon says: 'The dogs always get

47

*Louise Wilson at RAF
Sealand with sniffer
Spaniel Twist*

excited at home if they see me put my uniform on. What other dogs get to spend all day with their owners? They love going to work. We don't have any really bad days. A bad day would be if a training exercise doesn't go well. Or you might get to a job and there are too many members of the public for the dog to be able to work, or you can't get a scent track because of contamination. But to find a missing person for example, is the best feeling in the world. We all live for the next dog job. Not surprisingly the dog unit is hard to get on to. We had forty people recently applying for a vacancy. I love being a police officer and I love dogs. The best thing is getting a result. Finding the evidence that has been missed. For example, my dog Saxon, who has recently retired, did some fantastic work a couple of months ago. A patrol called for help with two people they were suspicious about. They'd gone running off into a field, but the officers couldn't find the reason for their behaviour. But Saxon came and did a search of the area and found a bolt cutter and a pair of gloves. We wouldn't have found them without Saxon, and the two people were arrested.'

Sniffer Spaniel Twist

Rather than breeding their own dogs, Kent Police prefer to train rescued dogs or those donated by the public, but each dog handler trains his own dog, with the help of trainer PC Neil Mullett. PC Mullett introduced me to a young working Cocker who had just been donated by his breeder: 'His name is Cobb and he is sixteen months old. Hopefully he will learn to sniff out explosives, and now we are just checking to see if he has a natural aptitude.' As Cobb flew off to exactly where the 'explosive' was hidden, PC Mullett said: 'He looks like he is going to be OK. He just wants to work and work. We have another Cocker in training as well, they tend to have the outgoing, bold temperament we need. Nothing ever phases him. As we train, Cobb's reward is usually to play fetch with the tennis ball, which we throw for him if he succeeds in sniffing out the explosive. We do use food rewards as well in some of the training, particularly where we are training for blood scent. Where we can't have them destroying the evidence.'

PC Paul Diddams's dog Windsor, a German Shepherd general purpose dog, has just started training to be a forensics dog, sniffing for tiny specks of blood that even crime scene investigators can miss. Recently Windsor was able to help in the case of a victim who had just been stabbed, but couldn't – or wouldn't – say where it had happened. Windsor came out and started searching on the road and found the blood and tracked it back to the man's home, where PC Diddams found the victim's partner, who had done the stabbing.

The results of one of Windsor's best pieces of work have just gone through the courts. Neil Loudon describes the case: 'We got a call that there was a robbery going on at a large jewellery store. We got the helicopter involved and got the car stopped and the men ran out. They left the jewellery behind, but we lost them. Then Paul turned up with Windsor and started tracking. The area was contaminated with all sorts of smells, but Paul and Windsor continued and spent a couple of hours searching. Then Windsor found one of the offenders hiding in a bush. Windsor barked at the bush, and the offender gave himself up. But then the man changed his mind and ran off again and so Windsor gave chase and got a hold on him. The offender started fighting him, but Windsor held on and the arrest was made.

'All the time we are discovering what the dogs can do. Our dogs are really well used, in demand constantly. The general purpose dogs often help in searching for lost people – sometimes a confused elderly person or a child. We had a wonderful success recently, by PC Stuart Fotheringham and his dog Brinx. A young child had gone missing from home and we were all out looking. Patrols had already searched the house so everybody was beginning to get worried, but Stuart decided to put Brinx into the house to have a search – and Brinx found the child hiding in a cupboard under a pile of bedclothes. That was a great result, most importantly we found the child quickly, but also we were able to call off what would have been a very expensive search with helicopters and a lot of resources.'

This ability of dogs to find people hidden in tiny spaces is especially valuable for the UK Border Agency, who have the job of patrolling Britain's borders for everything from illegal immigrants to contraband goods – and use more than sixty dogs to help them do it. Dog unit manager Wes Fernandez explains: 'Many of our dogs are actually based over in France so that they can check vehicles and lorries in Calais and Dunkirk before they even get to the UK. The dogs do a terrific job, we have more than twenty of them based over in France with their handlers. From a tax payer's perspective, illegal immigrants are a major cost to the country. But what is often overlooked is the humanitarian aspect of the job. People take risks by crawling into chilled container lorries or confined spaces, and there have been deaths in the past. We have some dogs who have found dozens of people – and saved their lives by doing so.'

Sniffer dog searching a lorry for the UK Border Agency

Foremost among these is Lola, a three-year-old German Short-Haired Pointer who found twenty-four illegal immigrants in just one week. In a recent find she dragged her handler, James Niven, for fifty yards to get to a lorry driving into Calais ferry terminal, barking to indicate her suspicions. James said: 'She dragged me down there because she got a big whiff of the scent.' Sure enough, when the border officials searched the German lorry, they found a Vietnamese teenage boy and girl and an older man, hidden among air-conditioning parts. The immigrants had spent nine hours crushed into the tiny gap between the lorry's cargo and its roof after stowing away in the south of France. Any longer in the confined space could have been life-threatening. But luckily for them, Lola was on watch that day, and according to James: 'Lola is 100 per cent successful if she catches any scent. She always comes up trumps.'

Sniffing for explosives in London on the Thames embankment

Collin Singer's company WagtailUK found and trained Lola, and Collin explained why her success was so pleasing: 'With Lola I had a call from a lady whose pub had had to go out of business due to the recession, so she couldn't keep Lola any more – but now Lola's done so well there is a happy ending to the story. Quite a lot of our dogs we get from rescue centres and they have not had the best of times. Recently we accepted a dog, Sam, from the Blue Cross and he's doing well in his training and will soon be ready to go over and work in France. I think we were the fourth potential new home they had tried, so Sam hadn't had the best of luck, but now he's found his niche with us and really enjoying life.

'The dogs really love their work. They can be trained to search for all sorts of different things – firearms, explosives, drugs, cash, tobacco, humans. Our theory is that if it has got a scent you can train a dog to detect it. The basic principle is converting the dog's natural instinct into a game, so the dog searches and then gets rewarded by playing with its favourite toy. We make sure to select the dogs carefully to have a natural desire to play and a willingness to learn and to work – the gundog breeds are excellent in this respect. A Spaniel, for example, will be crazy for its ball, and we extend that into a game of hide and seek and eventually into detecting people hidden in lorries. We make it easy and fun at first, and you soon reach the point where the dog is happily searching 100

Dogs can be taught almost any scent, here Twister is detecting bats

Collin Singer and colleague Louise Wilson of Wagtail UK with a recent find © *Wagtail UK*

lorries. Once they are working in a real situation though, there is an added element which is that the surrounding environment may be noisy, busy, distracting or even slightly stressful and you need a dog that can cope with that.'

Collin is very proud of his dogs, who work all over the world for a number of different organisations, both governmental and private: 'Recently one of our dogs working for the UK Border Agency found eighteen people hiding in a tanker full of gluten powder. They had to lift the top hatches to get them out, and the people were crammed in this tiny space at the top of the load, all covered in this white powdery stuff. That could have been a disaster if they hadn't been found. And we find people doing even more dangerous things – clinging to the underneath of a lorry that's going to be doing fifty mph in freezing conditions.' It's great to know that a dog overlooked by everyone else can go on to have a fulfilling career as a hero dog, often saving human lives.

above *A helicopter search by Wagtail UK*

Sniffer dog Paddy searches a Boeing airshow chalet

*Louise Wilson with
drugs search dog, Meg*

below *Luna searches
for traces of rare pine
martens*

"First, they do an on-line search."

CHAPTER THREE

EVERY DOG'S LASSIE MOMENT

The Pet Dogs Who Have Discovered their Inner Hero

Have you ever looked at your dog, as he fools around on your morning walk, and wondered what he would do if the chips were down? If you were being chased by escaped bank robbers, would he run in and fight them off? Or perhaps if you were hanging by your fingernails off a cliff, could he grab your sleeve and haul you to safety? Most of all, if you uttered the immortal command: 'Lassie, get help!' – would he? Lassie was a fictional Collie dog created by Eric Knight in his short-story *Lassie Come-Home,* published as a novel in 1940. The idea of a boy and his wonderfully intelligent collie companion captured the public imagination, and a whole string of films and a long-running television series followed.

In real life Eric Knight is believed to have been influenced by a story he heard about a Collie-cross called Lassie who saved a mariner's life during World War I. Lassie was owned by the landlord of a pub called The Pilot Boat in Lyme Regis. On New Year's Day 1915, HMS *Formidable* was hit by a torpedo from a German submarine off the south Devon

coast and sank. More than 500 men were lost, but some made it onto life rafts. One of the rafts was washed ashore in Lyme Bay. Rescuers brought its unconscious occupants into the pub, where the dead were laid out on tables. But Lassie kept licking the face and feet of one of the sailors, Able-Seaman John Cowan, gradually bringing him round. Luckily someone noticed that John was reacting, and his life was saved.

The stories in this book make it clear that the tale of the original Lassie is far from improbable. Dogs today are detecting cancer; predicting epileptic seizures; or monitoring blood sugar levels on a daily basis all over Britain and the rest of the world. Search and rescue dogs are regularly finding buried survivors in disaster zones. And even the more dramatic adventures of the fictional Lassie on film are repeatedly replicated by real life dogs. But most of the dogs featured have been specially bred and trained to perform their amazing feats. Surely ordinary pet dogs couldn't be so heroic? This chapter proves the opposite. Maureen Burns's pet red Collie-cross dog, Max, alerted her to cancer by nudging and licking her breast, in an almost carbon-copy of the original Lassie story. And dogs recreating the exploits of the fictional Lassie make the headlines every year.

In the summer of 2011, Sergeant Lorraine Roberts, from Devon and Cornwall Police, couldn't believe what she saw when she was called to an accident on the rocks above Torquay's Meadfoot Beach. She said: 'It was just like a scene from a Lassie film. There was a couple lying injured out of sight below the cliff-edge, while the dog ran up and down like a mad thing, barking furiously.' The team who rescued a middle-aged couple from seventy-five feet down the cliff-face, immediately nicknamed the couple's spaniel 'Lassie' for the way in which it alerted them to the spot by barking, and then refused to leave its owners. David Kimberley was enjoying a cliff-top walk when he was one of the first to be aware of the emergency. He describes the spaniel's actions: 'She kept running about and jumped down over the small wall at the top of the cliff road until finally someone realised what had happened.' But when the coastguard arrived they had a job to get 'Lassie' back to the top herself – by then she'd climbed down further and wouldn't leave her owners. Coastguard Dave Chilcott said: 'The rescue was relatively simple, but getting Lassie to the top proved a bit more difficult. We kept throwing slices of ham closer and closer and gradually she came up the cliff. She was certainly the heroine of the hour.'

Fortunately this dog was saved, but some dogs go as far as to give up their own lives to save humans. In April 2007, Alan Gay's fifteen-year-old Jack Russell terrier, George, was out walking with his neighbour's children when two pit bull terriers, running loose, came up behind them. The pit bulls went into attack mode and the children were soon in serious danger, but George wasn't having it. He ran repeatedly at the dogs, barking vigorously as they closed in on him. It gave the children time to get away, but as an old dog, George couldn't recover from his injuries. His bravery won't be forgotten though, as he was posthumously awarded the PDSA Gold Medal – the animal equivalent of the George Cross.

Another Gold Medal winner, Bosnich (known to his friends as Bos), discovered his inner Lassie in August 2006, when accompanying his owner Lorna Farish's father, Mark, on a walk in Cumbria. Mark Corrie,

seventy-three, and Bos set off on their regular walk in Gelt Woods, near Brampton, Cumbria. But when Mark was overdue to arrive home, Lorna called the police. The police, with their own search dogs, and mountain rescue volunteers, searched for two days without success. Just as they were beginning to give up, a group of local walkers heard a dog howling on the south side of Cumrew Fell, about seven miles from Brampton. They rushed to check it out and spotted Bos from the top of a ridge. As soon as he saw them, Bos changed his howl to a persistent, attention demanding bark, and then he managed to lead the walkers to where Mark Corrie was lying. Mark was cold, confused and suffering from dehydration, but luckily not seriously hurt. As everybody waited for the emergency services Bos never moved from Mark's side, lying close to him to give additional warmth. Penrith Mountain Rescue Team reported: 'Without Bos keeping the pensioner warm and his determined howling and barking Mark Corrie might not have been found.'

Terrier, George, fended off two pit bull terriers
© PDSA

Bosnich directed rescuers to where Mark Corrie had fallen © PDSA

Many companion dogs have been honoured for actions far beyond what could be expected of a 'civilian' dog. Wheelchair-bound student Cheryl Smith was out with her Golden Retriever Orca for an afternoon in the countryside in the summer of 2003 when Cheryl's powered wheelchair hit a rock and threw Cheryl sideways down a fifteen-foot embankment into a water-filled ditch. Her wheelchair landed on top of Cheryl, pinning her face-down in the icy rainwater. But Cheryl was able to shout up to Orca to 'get help'. She lay there hoping for the best,

Assistance dog Orca fetched help for Cheryl Smith
© PDSA

while Orca disappeared – on what turned out to be his own epic adventure. The first person Orca came across ignored his frantic attempts to communicate and just assumed he was some sort of stray. Orca found himself being 'rescued' when he was in the middle of a rescue himself! Eventually he was able to break free from the makeshift lead and dash off to try and find someone else, before more valuable time was lost. Luckily the next person Orca met was Cheryl's neighbour, Peter Harrison, out jogging. Peter recognised Orca and quickly followed him back along a canal towpath until they got to where Cheryl was lying in the ditch and Peter was able to get emergency services to help pull her out.

Gulf War veteran Allen Parton had a similar experience with his Canine Partner dog, Endal. Naval engineer, Allen, had suffered brain injuries during the Gulf War in 1991, leaving him initially unable to walk, speak, read, write or remember his past. When Endal came into his life, he immediately inspired Allen with the enthusiasm to start re-habilitation. Endal and Allen were soon inseparable, which was just as well, because in the spring of 2001 Allen was knocked out of his wheel-chair in a hotel car park and left unconscious on the ground. There was no one around, but Endal did not panic. Instead, he calmly manoeu-vred Allen into the recovery position, covered him with a blanket from

Assistance dog, Endal, put his owner in the recovery position © PDSA

the wheelchair and pushed the mobile to Allen's face. Only when Allen regained consciousness did Endal leave his side to summon help.

These are all dogs who were not found wanting when the call came. But what about dogs who are deliberately put into risky situations by their explorer or adventurer owners? Sled dog racer Alan Stewart, of Cairngorm Sleddog Centre, near Aviemore in Scotland's Cairngorm mountains, is the first to admit that what he asks his dogs to do can be dangerous. 'I have competed in the snowy and high places all over the world,' he says. 'There are no trails or routes. When you go into an environment like that and you are asking your dog to come too, you both have to be very sure of what you are doing.' Luckily for Alan he found the dog of a lifetime, Buster, who would be there for him in many tight spots over the years. Surprisingly Buster wasn't a Husky dog at all, but a pet German Short-Haired Pointer. 'I found an advert, this guy who was giving his dog away. The guy owned a chain of restaurants and lived in the middle of London, so I flew down from Scotland. The second that I came in I could see this young seven-month-old pointer was in the

Buster and team

wrong environment.' Alan knew the pup needed the wide-open spaces of the Scottish Highlands, and so Buster began life as a lead sled dog.

'Buster and I did thousands of miles together,' remembers Alan. 'There were no sled dog genes in him but no matter what the pressure on him as lead dog, he never once bottled out. He was the first UK dog to do the big sled races in Europe. We were on these horrendous mountains, 3,000 metres up on the Alpen trail. I had crampons on and even the Huskies were slipping and sliding. If Buster had turned round the team we would all have fallen but Buster never put a paw wrong. He is still the only sled dog to have gone across the Cairngorm Mountains – it was just Buster and me sledding through the Llarig Ghru from Braemar to Aviemore. It was twenty degrees below freezing, and he came into my sleeping bag with me.'

Of course, not all pet dogs do come up trumps. Some clearly just do not have an inner Lassie – as Sir Edward Dashwood was forced to conclude with his old Spaniel: 'The only useful thing she ever did was land my fish for me when I was both trout and salmon fishing. She knew exactly what was going on and would sit about thirty yards downstream of me watching my fly intently. At least it saved me carrying a net!' Another aristocratic canine was the Duke of Northumberland's German Wire-Haired Pointer, Kruger, who had a classic 'Lassie' moment: 'Kruger had a great bond with my son's Cocker Spaniel, Stan,' remembers the Duke. 'One day we'd all been out for a long walk and didn't notice until we arrived home, that Stan was missing. Kruger, on the other hand, was frantic with worry and insisted that we follow him back down the track, with him stopping every now and then to make sure we were following. Eventually he led us through the undergrowth to a sheep fence and there, trapped on the other side, was young Stan waiting to be rescued.'

Dogs rescuing other dogs is a far from unusual occurrence. One day I was walking with my dog, Dutch, and a Cocker puppy, April, alongside the River Tay in Scotland. As puppies will, April jumped into the swirling brown waters of a river in full flood, and soon got into difficulties. Just as I was about to go in to rescue her, Dutch beat me to it. He dived in, swimming strongly against the current, and reached April, where he trailed his long spaniel's ear past her nose. She grabbed it between her teeth, and he dragged her back to the bank.

I didn't believe I had interpreted the incident correctly until a dog-trainer friend, Anne Heading, from Scotland, recounted a similar story: 'I was walking along the beach in Aberdeenshire with a friend and our dogs – I had my young Labrador, Ranger, and he had brought his young Cocker, Monty, who was on his first visit to the seaside. We were chatting at the water's edge and my friend threw a stone in to see if Monty would swim in the waves. Monty didn't hesitate for a second, but took off at great speed and cut through the sea like an Olympic champion, swimming as if intent on reaching Norway by teatime! No amount of whistling could get him to turn, and we were beginning to get seriously alarmed he would be caught in a current. Then all of a sudden, without any command, Ranger threw himself into the ocean and powered out after Monty. When he reached the little Cocker, he turned in front of him and steered him back towards the shore.'

What is extraordinary about most of the 'Lassie moments' described here, is that the dogs are working on their own initiative. Many of the owners comment that the dog just seemed to know what to do all on its own. Paraplegic former police officer, Simon Anderson from Somerset, is still amazed by this aspect of dogs' behaviour, even twelve years on from his German Short-Haired Pointer discovering her inner Lassie. 'I think we underestimate our pet dogs,' says Simon: 'They have faculties that we can only guess at.' Simon had a serious accident on his police patrol bike in 1999, which left him hospitalised for more than a year. A couple of years earlier he and his wife,

Simon Anderson with Tiley and friends

Claire, had taken on their first dog, a German Short-Haired Pointer pup called Fudge. Simon remembers: 'Eventually I was allowed to have a visit from Fudge. She couldn't come into the ward, but I was wheeled in my bed into the lounge where she was waiting. She hadn't seen me for three

Claire Anderson and Olga

months, but it was the most amazing thing – when she jumped on to the bed, she did a special thing with her front paws folded underneath. I had pins and casts and whatnot, and was in a hell of a state, so she folded her paws back out of the way without any instruction. How did she know to do that?'

This was just the beginning of Fudge's intuitive response to Simon's new, and very different set of needs from her. Simon says: 'When I eventually came home, Fudge adapted very quickly. She would pick up all sorts of objects that I wanted, and then bring over to me. She would summon help and would carry stuff like money or a phone for me. Paraplegics like myself are prone to getting urinary tract infections, and Fudge knew at least twenty-four hours before I did if I was going down with one and would warn me by going to my side and sticking there. Even once I was laid up in bed, Fudge would stay by my side throughout. My wife, Claire, would have to come and take her out for her food and to go to the lavatory.

'The more time we spent together the more she became dialled in to my physical condition and the things I needed. Where does it all start? It leaves you wondering how they do it. People say humans read too much into what a dog is thinking or doing, but Fudge has proved herself beyond doubt time and again.' Inspired by Fudge, Simon has started giving talks about his experiences and has raised thousands of pounds for the Support Dogs charity, which trains dogs to perform tasks specifically tailored to the needs of their disabled owner, as well as training dogs which can alert to seizure and other medical emergencies.

Maureen Burns's pet Collie-cross, Max, needed no training to alert her to an upcoming medical emergency. At first Maureen, from Rugby, Warwickshire, was worried it was Max who was ill: 'Max was acting sad, he'd stopped being this hyper dog that I knew so well. We'd rescued him from the RSPCA as a youngster, and he was nine-years-old, and I thought maybe it was age – even though that's not that old.' Maureen had had a non-cancerous lump known as a fibro adenoma removed from her breast some years before, so was always conscientious about checking her breasts. 'Then one day, I remember it so clearly, I was checking my breasts in the mirror and Max was lying on the bed behind me. By this time he wouldn't sit beside my feet as he normally did. He had always been my soul mate. Now he would come and sniff my breath and occasionally he would nose my breast. I saw the reflection in the mirror of Max on the bed and our eyes met and I could tell instantly.

Maureen Burns's pet Collie-cross, Max

'I went to the doctors and got referred to the hospital and they sent me straight down for a mammogram and scan. But they couldn't find anything. It wasn't detectable on either, but the surgeon could feel a lump and so he did five biopsies. Just one of them showed slightly suspect, so he did seven more – and the results came through, and two showed cancer. After I came home from surgery, from that moment Max was back to normal – wagging his tail and back to his old self. But I had never heard of anything like this happening. I happened to mention it to the breast care nurse and she wasn't at all surprised. She said, "I've heard about this before." That was such a relief for me – I thought I'm not imagining it, I'm not mad, it does happen!'

In fact there is now a whole science of cancer detection and medical alert by dogs. Two groups, Cancer & Bio-detection Dogs and Medical Alert Dogs, have come together under the umbrella charitable organisation, Medical Detection Dogs, which is making huge strides in researching dogs' abilities, and putting them to practical use. Maureen is a keen supporter of the Charity: 'I have now had a chance to watch the trained dogs working. The samples are on this big carousel and the dogs go round and sniff each sample, and they sit down to indicate if

Maureen Burns with her pet dog Max, who detected her breast cancer

they have found a cancerous sample. They are rewarded for sniffing it out and a ball is thrown, so it isn't like it was for Max. I will never forget the look Max gave me that day – dogs can have very expressive faces and his was so sad; it was a look of great pity. I'm not exaggerating. These days Max still checks me out before I go for a follow-up appointment. He is thirteen now and getting rather deaf and arthritic, but he's fine. I think what I have really learnt from this experience is that the sky's the limit; I believe we have really been underestimating the potential of what dogs can achieve.'

CHAPTER FOUR

HUNTING HIGH AND LOW

The Volunteer Search and Rescue Dogs

M OUNTAIN RESCUERS TRY not to be judgemental, but the advice they always give hill walkers is to go out properly equipped – by which they mean sensible walking boots and a map you can understand, rather than trainers and a mobile phone! When the inevitable SOS goes out, the one bit of 'equipment' the rescuers wouldn't be without is a dog. The UK's National Search And Rescue Dog Association (NSARDA) is the umbrella group for a number of different SARDA groups all over England, Scotland, Wales and Northern Ireland, providing volunteer search dog teams not just for mountain rescues but also general searches for missing people here in the UK and all over the world.

By September of 2011 SARDA in England had already been called out on eighty-seven different searches, and expect to be called out more than 150 times a year. Many of the call-outs are false alarms, or happily the missing person turns up under their own steam. But sadly some of the searches will result in the dog finding someone who hasn't survived. The best moment for the searchers and their dogs is when they can make a rescue and save a life. Up in the Peak District, Toby and his owner Paul

Making a 'find' during
snow training
© SARDAWales

below **SARDA England**
team commence a search
© George Ledger Photography/
SARDA England

SARDA England team prepares to join a helicopter search
© George Ledger Photography/ SARDA England

Taylor had a wonderfully uplifting summer in 2011, finding ten walkers and helping them home. In May Paul and Toby were among three dog teams searching Edale for five teenagers on a practice walk for the Duke of Edinburgh's Award. Night had fallen while they were still out on the hill, but Toby quickly found them, and Paul was pleased to see that the youngsters had sensibly got themselves under shelter and waited for help. Toby's next find, the following month, was of a young man who'd wandered off on the moor, but luckily was well enough to continue his walk under his own steam once Toby had shown him the way. More worrying was a search in August for an elderly couple out walking, who'd managed to call in to say they were lost. The couple were thrilled when Toby came bounding up to them, and Paul was then able to help them get back home. Only a few days later Paul and Toby had a similar call out, this time from a father and son walking the Pennine Way together. Darkness had taken the pair by surprise, but Paul and Toby soon tracked them down – a busy but rewarding summer!

Not far away in the Yorkshire Dales, search dogs were having a dramatic time. In early spring an SOS went out that a light aircraft had crashed in dense fog on the moors at Ingleborough. Two dog teams

SARDA England Collie, Hollie, about to make a find © *George Ledger Photography/SARDA England*

rushed to the area and started searching. Bill Batson and his dog Glen found the wrecked aircraft and its two occupants just after midnight. Both men had survived the crash but were injured. If they hadn't been found quickly the outlook would have been bleak, with hypothermia being the biggest danger as the men lay unable to move on the edge of the remote Ingleborough summit. The men had to be stretchered for over a mile off the hill to get to vehicles, and then safely off to hospital.

SARDA's North-East region had a tough search in the winter of 2011, looking for a man out walking on the high Pennines. Having found the man's car fairly easily, they then had to search a large area of mountain including the Cross Fell area, and part of the Pennine Way. By now it was dark, but search dog Nut found a scent and indicated it. Nut then kept searching, repeatedly finding the trail of the missing man, but confusingly the trail seemed to go in circles. Nut was crossing and re-crossing Trout Beck. He stuck to it, making longer and wider searches each time

74

he came across the scent and finally his persistence was rewarded. The lost man heard Nut's barks coming nearer and nearer and was able to shout for help. It turned out the walker had got himself thoroughly lost. Nut's confusing search had actually been following his exact path as he had crossed and re-crossed the beck. Surprisingly this walker had prepared himself a map and compass, but the vital ingredient – a torch to read them – was missing!

SARDA Scotland is kept just as busy as the English groups, with the additional problems of some of Britain's highest and most exposed upland areas, constantly used by walkers, climbers, serious mountaineers and even skiers. They carry out between eighty and 100 searches annually, divided up among about twenty-five different dog and handler teams. SARDA Scotland has been making rescues for half a century. The famous Alpine and Himalayan mountaineer, Hamish Macinnes, got the idea for search dogs when he was climbing in the Alps. He had visited an avalanche dog training course in Switzerland in the early 1960s, and brought the concept back home to Scotland – where he is still President SARDA Scotland. SARDA Scotland secretary Moira Weatherstone explains: 'All our handlers are volunteers who are on call twenty-four hours a day. They all do a marvellous job but our real heroes are our dogs.'

SARDA's Ireland North call-out and training co-ordinator, Neil Palmer, agrees with Moira: 'I have been involved in search and rescue for more than forty years and have had twelve wonderful dogs over that time who've all made the most amazing rescues. These dogs burrow their way into your heart. As a trainer I do a lot of behavioural work with difficult dogs and I tell everyone that dogs are not less than humans, they are just different from humans, and that is my firm conviction. I don't like to see people dressing up pet dogs like humans – it's disrespectful. I have eight dogs at home just now, and they all have their own personalities – to be honest I would prefer them to most people.'

This isn't surprising, considering the extraordinary rescues Neil's dogs have made all over the world. Recently Neil has added a Bloodhound-cross called Paddy to the team: 'I have only just completed his training as a trailing dog,' explained Neil, 'but we used him the other night. There was a lady who went missing from her home and after two days of fruitless searching, the police rang me to ask if the Bloodhound could help. It was at the very limit of Paddy's ability – a fifty-hour old trail after rain and high winds. The girl had left her car and it had been found in the early hours of Saturday. I asked the police for some articles of clothing and used a t-shirt to give the scent to Paddy. We were on a busy road, but he picked up the trail and away we went for a mile and a quarter to a wall at the edge of a cliff. Then Paddy set off again and went another fifty yards and found a gap in the wall and tried to pull me through it. He was going mad, trying to get down there and forty feet down there was a ledge where it was clear someone had gone over. I was amazed by Paddy's ability so early in his training. It is really extra-ordinary what the dogs can do.'

Neil Palmer with his first search dog, Pepper

Another of Neil's dogs, a Labrador called Charco, was luckier in the results of his recent search: 'He has been working with me recently in earthquakes in Algeria and Kashmir – where he managed to find a man alive who had been buried for thirty-six hours. Charco was able to show us where he was, and an international team managed to dig the guy out, with the ground still trembling all around us.'

Neil's very first dog, Pepper, was one of his best: 'He found a German scout who had been lost for thirty-six hours in the mountain in Donegal. The child had been searched for and no one had found him. Then Pepper found this little drain high in the mountains and he indicated to a piece of tarpaulin lying in the ditch. I thought, 'Pepper, you've let me down here,' but I lifted the end of the tarpaulin and there was this little eleven-year-old boy. He'd been too weak to call out – it was brilliant to find him.'

Two of Neil's dogs have received PDSA Gold Medals for their courageous work. Neil explains how Dylan

Neil Palmer's search dogs, Dylan and Cracker

won his award: 'There were four Duke of Edinburgh Award kids who had gone missing in the Mourne Mountains for a long time in bad weather. There had already been people in the search area, which made scenting difficult – plus the visibility was only fifteen metres and there were high winds and rain. Dylan tended to work in big loops out and round me, and this time he was gone for a good ten minutes and I didn't know where he was. Then he appeared out of the mist, barking like hell and then just turned round and disappeared back into the mist. He waited for me to catch up, and we repeated this a few times, climbing up over ledges and boulders. Eventually he got me to the spot, there were the four kids, alive but trapped on the ledge. That was a fantastic achievement.

'Dylan's brother, Cracker, got his gold medal for work in Turkey. It was a terrible earthquake, and he had been searching for hours. There was this fine powdery dust everywhere and Cracker was exhausted and finding it difficult to breath. We were washing out his nostrils and resting with some of the survivors, including a family, who were terribly

Dylan and Cracker receive their PDSA Gold Medals
© PDSA

upset. The interpreter explained their daughter was still missing in the family home. So we went over to it, and the building was completely compacted, it was horrendous. Cracker was so tired, I thought it would be too much for him, but he worked his way through the tangle of debris. Then he came back and his body language told me: "I'm afraid there's no one alive there, Dad." The people were very grateful for the help, at least they could start grieving.'

Sadly, the outcome of many searches is a sad one for humans and dogs, but Lou Holmes, from Berkshire, who specialises in lowland searches, explains that there is a positive side even then: 'When that is the outcome, there are three things to remember. Firstly, every person that we go looking for has been reported missing by somebody – so no matter what has happened it shows that somebody has cared enough and wants to know where that person is. Another big thing for me is that search and rescue teams are trained to cope, even if it is grim when we make the find. We have the support systems, whereas a civilian who finds the body of a loved one is not going to cope – it is the worst possible outcome for the family to be the ones who find. And most importantly, by finding, even in tragic circumstances, we are at least bringing closure to the family and allowing the grieving process to start. I can think of nothing worse than not knowing.'

Lou and her dog, Brock, a Collie-cross, had to confront these issues very early on in their search and rescue career, when Brock was the dog to find the body of Dr David Kelly, the MoD weapons expert embroiled in the Iraq invasion controversy. Lou remembers: 'Dr Kelly went missing not very long after Brock and I had started performing searches. Brock was the first dog I had trained as a search dog, and he was the first qualified lowland search and rescue dog. He learned very quickly and was only seven months old when he qualified.

Lou Holmes's lowland search dog, Brock © The Kennel Club Friends for Life

'Our very first search had been just before Christmas, when an elderly gentleman had gone missing near Reading and it was the first time dogs had been used in a lowland environment, so it was nerve wracking. There was me and Brock and a support person and four or five police officers observing. Brock went off searching and ran down a very steep bank and into a rhododendron bush at the bottom and barked. So we all had to scramble down this horrid mucky bank, and it turned out to be just a football! Fortunately they saw the funny side. Then fairly soon afterwards, we got called to a search near Bicester to look for a young lad who had left a suicide note and fortunately it was Brock's indication that eventually led to his being discovered. After that the police started to believe in us and that was a big turning point. And then a few days later Dr Kelly went missing and we were called in.

'With Brock it had quite an effect on him when he found Dr Kelly. The dog knows if the person is dead, and even as we started searching we did think Dr Kelly would probably be dead. Brock found the body and came back to me and barked and then just turned round and stared at where he had come from rather than running back. So I knew there was something there different. For a few weeks Brock was reluctant to

Waiting at the mountain rescue rendezvous
© SARDA Wales

Fly takes a high position in Snowdonia
© SARDA Wales

A SARDA England Collie in the Peak District © *George Ledger Photography/SARDA England*

go back to people in training, but he quickly got over it. All the people in our team that have found a dead person noticed a bit of change in the dog's behaviour.

'With the Dr Kelly case I had to give evidence in court. That was eight years ago but every year we are still door-stepped by journalists because of the Hutton Inquiry. Brock and I were given a Chief Constable's commendation, making Brock the only dog ever to have had a Chief Constable's commendation. So I'm proud of that, and glad to have been able to help Dr Kelly's family. Since then we have been able to show what the dogs can do. In the last ten days alone we have been called out eleven times. Very recently we had a call out which involved several different dog teams on a big four day search. Eventually we found the man alive, after he'd been out missing for four nights and that was a wonderful feeling.'

And if it is rewarding for the dogs and their owners to find someone who is lost and stranded – just imagine how wonderful it is for a person who is found, to hear joyful barking and feel a welcoming (if wet) doggy nose snuffling at your face!

Resting after a training day © *George Ledger Photography/SARDA England*

A helicopter brings Cluanie into the search area © SARDA Wales

below *Cluanie landed safely and starts searching* © SARDA Wales

Cluanie taking a break during a search at Tremadaog © SARDA Wales

Labrador pups being familiarised with search activities © SARDA Wales

A new Collie puppy joins SARDA Wales © SARDA Wales

SARDA England Collie in training © George Ledger Photography/SARDA England

CHAPTER FIVE

'FOR GALLANTRY'

The Stories of Dogs Honoured for their Bravery

Anyone driving along London's Park Lane since 2004 will have noticed the dramatic 'Animals in War' Memorial at the Brook Gate to Hyde Park, celebrating the heroism of animals serving in wartime. The memorial shows two heavily laden army pack mules struggling through a small gap in a huge wall made from Portland stone. On the other side of the wall a carthorse and a dog, unrestricted by harnesses, walk free from the turmoil and cast a backward glance towards their comrades who haven't made it. The Animals in War Memorial is so moving, reminding us of all the times and ways in which we have pressed animals into our service.

In the last century it was horses above all who served, with a tragic loss of life. Eight million horses and countless mules and donkeys died in World War I. Even in World War II, mules and horses were still being used, especially to transport ammunition and supplies through otherwise impassable terrain. Surprisingly to some, pigeons played a huge role in both world wars, with more than 200,000 flying with honour in World War II. The Animals in War Memorial trust explains: 'The pigeons performed heroically and saved thousands of lives by carrying vital messages, sometimes over long distances, when other methods of communication were impossible. Flying at the rate of a mile a minute from the front line, from behind enemy lines or from ships or aeroplanes, these gallant birds would struggle on through all weathers, even when severely wounded and exhausted, in order to carry their vital messages home.'

During times of war the most unlikely animals have played a role. Working animals like elephants, camels and oxen carried out tasks similar to those they had been performing before the outbreak of war. But more unusual participants were canaries, glow worms and cats! One of the memorial's major supporters, the Duke of Westminster, explains that it is important to remember them all: 'So many animals served, suffered and died in the wars and this memorial is a fitting tribute to them.'

As you might expect, dogs didn't let themselves be left out when it came to serving their country. Clarissa Baldwin, Chief Executive of the Dogs Trust, says: 'We have so many stories of the fantastic deeds that dogs performed on behalf of the Services during the war, so it is right there should be a lasting tribute to their courage, intelligence and bravery.' The memorial trust highlights that dogs are both devoted and intelligent, explaining: 'Among their many duties, these faithful animals ran messages, laid telegraph wires, detected mines, dug out bomb victims and acted as guard or patrol dogs. Many battled on despite horrific wounds and in terrifying circumstances to the limit of their endurance, showing indomitable courage and supreme loyalty to their handlers.'

The legend on the memorial reads: 'They had no choice.' In the case of dogs, and what makes their actions even more heroic, is that they did have a choice – yet they still chose to do what they did. All dog lovers know that it's impossible to force a dog to do something or obey a command if it really doesn't want to. Dogs have all sorts of ways of getting out of it. They can cower and belly crawl, or run away or even display aggression. You simply can't command a dog to pick up a live grenade and take it away to safety. You can't force a dog to go in repeatedly and attack an enemy in order to defend the lives of its fellow human soldiers.

So the dogs who perform these acts are true hero dogs: they do it of their own free will, and often on their own initiative.

Since World War II they and other animals have received their own recognition for bravery in the form of the PDSA Dickin Medal, the animals' equivalent of the Victoria Cross. The medal is named after Maria Dickin, who founded the People's Dispensary for Sick Animals in 1917, starting with a free dispensary for sick animals in London's Whitechapel. Maria's ambition was to have mobile dispensaries travelling all over the country to relieve the suffering of animals whose owners were too poor to care for them. By 1923 there were sixteen PDSA dispensaries and Maria had also opened her first dispensary overseas in Tangiers – she had even designed a motor caravan dispensary. Eventually Maria Dickin was able to spread the PDSA all over the world, and opened the first ever sanatorium dedicated to animal health. Today the PDSA is as busy as ever, providing more than two million free treatments every year to sick and injured pets and more than 360,000 preventive treatments. Funded entirely by public support, the charity's UK PetAid hospitals cost about £53 million annually to run.

So far the PDSA has awarded the Dickin Medal just sixty-three times, with fifty-four of those medals related to acts of bravery during and in the aftermath of World War II. The most recent recipient of the medal is Treo, an eight-year-old Labrador-cross who joined the forces as an Arms Explosive Dog (AES dog) when he was two. Handled by Sergeant Dave Heyhoe, Treo was on a tour of duty in Afghanistan in 2008. By then he was an experienced AES dog who had been on active service before, carrying out his job of searching for weapons and explosives in operational theatres. But this time Treo was going into the line of fire. In March 2008 he was deployed right into the heart of the dangerous Helmand Province to search for devices, weapons and munitions hidden by the Taliban.

Great loss of life among soldiers serving in Afghanistan has been caused by the notorious 'IEDs' – improvised explosive devices hidden along the highways soldiers have to use. By August Treo had already located a 'daisy chain' IED concealed at the edge of a path in Sangin.

The IED had been booby-trapped and would certainly have exploded into the infantry detachment who were just about to use the road. The following month Treo was in action again, this time locating another IED which saved 7 Platoon, The Royal Irish Regiment, from guaranteed casualties. Treo made it back to blighty at the end of his tour, and in February 2010, PDSA Patron Princess Alexandra, presented him with his Dickin Medal in a special ceremony held at the Imperial War Museum, London. The medal citation praised Treo's: 'Outstanding contribution to the army's efforts in Afghanistan, saving lives and inspiring confidence and morale in the soldiers around him.'

Sgt Dave Heyhoe and Dickin Medal winner, Treo © MOD

Treo isn't the first dog to have been honoured as a result of service in Afghanistan. In November 2005, Sadie, a Labrador, was on assignment from the Royal Army Veterinary Corps (RAVC) to the Royal Gloucestershire, Berkshire and Wiltshire Light Infantry who were serving in Kabul. Her role would be as an arms and explosive search dog – one she would fulfil better than anyone could imagine. On 14 November 2005 military personnel serving with NATO's International Security Assistance Force in Kabul were involved in two separate attacks. Sadie and her handler, Lance Corporal Yardley, were deployed to search for secondary explosive devices. Sadie soon gave a positive indication near a concrete blast wall. The multinational personnel from NATO were then moved to a safe distance. Despite the obvious danger Sadie and Lance Corporal Yardley completed their search. Sadie was right. At the site of her indication, bomb disposal operators made safe an explosive device. The bomb had been designed to inflict maximum injury. Back in the UK, Sadie received her Dickin Medal in February 2007. The citation read: 'Sadie's actions undoubtedly saved the lives of many civilians and soldiers.'

Another Royal Army Veterinary Corps dog to serve with distinction was Sam, a German Shepherd Dog who had been assigned to the Royal Canadian Regiment in Drvar during the conflict in Bosnia-Herzegovina. Sam eventually received his award in 2003, but his extraordinarily courageous acts happened back in the spring of 1998, when tensions in Bosnia had sparked into rioting. His medal citation describes how Sam showed unswerving devotion to duty repeatedly during the grim month of April: 'On 18 April Sam successfully brought down an armed man threatening the lives of civilians and Service personnel. On 24th April, while guarding a compound harbouring Serbian refugees, Sam's determined approach held off rioters until reinforcements arrived. This dog's true valour saved the lives of many servicemen and civilians during this time of human conflict.'

The next area of conflict for British forces soon afterwards was Iraq. And it was here that the actions of Buster, a Springer Spaniel, really sum up how we all feel about our hero dogs. Buster received his medal: 'For outstanding gallantry in March 2003 while assigned to the Duke of

Wellington's Regiment in Safwan, Southern Iraq. Arms and explosives search dog, Buster, located an arsenal of weapons and explosives hidden behind a false wall in a property linked with an extremist group. Buster is considered responsible for saving the lives of service personnel and civilians. Following the find, all attacks ceased and shortly afterwards troops replaced their steel helmets with berets.'

The majority of canine Dickin Medals have been won by dogs serving during World War II. Rob, a Collie (War Dog No. 471/332 Special Air Service) was probably the only dog ever to become a member of the SAS. In January 1945 he received the Dickin Medal for taking part in landings during the North African Campaign, and for his later service with a Special Air Unit in Italy as patrol and guard on small detachments lying-up in enemy territory. His presence with these parties saved many of them from discovery and subsequent capture or destruction. Rob made over twenty parachute descents.

Although he was the only 'secret service dog', Rob isn't the only parachuting dog. Brian, an Alsatian, was attached to the Parachute Battalion of the 13th Battalion Airborne Division. He received his medal in March 1947: 'He landed in Normandy with his battalion and, having done the requisite number of jumps, became a fully-qualified Paratrooper.' Nowadays the feats of these dogs are being emulated by today's search and rescue dogs, who are trained to be winched down from a helicopter or crane into situations otherwise completely inaccessible.

Another World War II canine hero was Rifleman Khan, an Alsatian serving with the 147. 6th Battalion Cameronians, who rescued L/Cpl Muldoon from drowning under heavy shell fire at the assault of Walcheren, November 1944. Service dogs are just as attached to their soldier owners as any family pet, and this was shown by the extraordinary story of Antis, an Alsatian owned by a Czech airman, who received his Dickin Medal in 1949. Antis had served with his master in both the French Air Force and the RAF between 1940 and 1945, first in North Africa and then in England. After the war the pair returned to Czechoslovakia, only to find themselves plunged into another crisis with the Communist take-over and the death of Jan Masaryk. As they were forced to flee over the mountains: 'Antis substantially helped his master's escape across the frontier.'

Away from the front line, but in terrible conditions, Judy, a Pointer, was imprisoned by the Japanese. Her Dickin Medal citation (1946) reads: 'For magnificent courage and endurance in Japanese prison camps, which helped to maintain morale among her fellow prisoners and also for saving many lives through her intelligence and watchfulness.' At the same time, but far away in Israel, Punch and Judy, both Boxers, saved the lives of two British officers by attacking an armed terrorist. Punch received four bullet wounds during the action.

Gander, the Newfoundland mascot of the Royal Rifles of Canada, received his award posthumously for saving the lives of Canadian infantrymen during the Battle of Lye Mun, Hong Kong Island, in 1941. His citation reads: 'On three documented occasions Gander … engaged the enemy … Twice Gander's attacks halted the enemy's advance and protected groups of wounded soldiers. In a final act of bravery, the war dog was killed in action gathering a grenade. Without Gander's intervention many more lives would have been lost in the assault.'

Gallantry is not confined to well-bred dogs. Bob was just a mongrel who was taken on board by the 6th Royal West Kent Regiment during World War II. He received his Dickin Medal on 24 March 1944: 'For constant devotion to duty with special mention of Patrol work at Green Hill, North Africa, while serving with the 6th Battalion Queens Own Royal West Kent Regt.' Another extraordinarily brave mongrel was Tich, an Egyptian stray adopted by the 1st Battalion King's Royal Rifle Corps, who received his medal in July 1949: 'For loyalty, courage and devotion to duty under hazardous conditions of war 1941 to 1945, while serving with the 1st King's Rifle Corps in North Africa and Italy.'

Shortly after the end of World War II, in 1947, Ricky, a Welsh Collie, was on mine clearance work on a canal bank at Nederweent, Holland: 'He found all the mines but during the operation one of them exploded. Ricky was wounded in the head but remained calm and kept at work. Had he become excited he would have been a danger to the rest of the section working nearby.'

With the end of World War II it would have been hoped that both dogs and soldiers could retire from active duty, but sadly, from then to the present day, there has never been a time when dogs haven't been on active service alongside their military handlers. German Shepherd, Lucky, was one of several dogs who worked against the fierce terrorist activities in Malaya between 1949 and 1952. She was an RAF tracker dog, and worked along with her canine colleagues Bobbie, Jasper and Lassie. The team was so successful that they were seconded to assist the Coldstream Guards, the 2nd Battalion Royal Scots Guards, and the Ghurkhas, where they displayed extraordinary determination and life-saving skills. Sadly, three of the dogs lost their lives in the line of duty; only Lucky survived to the end of the conflict. But their amazing story was commemorated in February 2007 when Lucky posthumously received the Dickin Medal on behalf of her team: 'For the outstanding gallantry and devotion to duty of the RAF Police anti-terrorist tracker dog team. … The dogs and their handlers were an exceptional team, capable of tracking and locating the enemy by scent despite unrelenting heat and an almost impregnable jungle.'

Lucky's work was an early example of what has today become a familiar part of dog work, whether in the military or civilian emergency services – that of preventing terrorist acts or coping with their aftermath. Several war time awards of the medal have pre-figured the need today for search and rescue dogs to work on bombed sites. During World War II, the PDSA's own Rescue Squad dog, a Wire-Haired Terrier called Beauty, was honoured: 'For being the pioneer dog in locating buried air-raid victims while serving with a PDSA Rescue Squad.' Dogs clearly showed an instinctive ability to perform this unpredictable work during the war, without there being time for them to receive special training. For example, Rip was only a mongrel stray who was picked up by the Civil Defence Squad at Poplar in London's East End, but in 1945 he became famous, winning the Dickin Medal: 'For locating many air-raid victims during the blitz of 1940.' A Collie called Peter also won his medal that same year for the same work.

Alsatians really shone when it came to picking their way through the smouldering rubble searching for signs of life. Civil defence dogs Jet and Irma, both Alsatians, received their medals: 'For being responsible for the rescue of persons trapped under blitzed buildings while serving with the Civil Defence Services of London.' And their colleague, Thorn, another Alsatian, won his medal: 'For locating air-raid casualties in spite of thick smoke in a burning building.' Even more determined was another of the civil defence's Alsatians, Rex, who showed: 'Outstanding good work in the location of casualties in burning buildings. Undaunted by smouldering debris, thick smoke, intense heat and jets of water from fire hoses, this dog displayed uncanny intelligence and outstanding determination in his efforts to follow up any scent which led him to a trapped casualty.'

The description of Rex's work is disturbingly like that carried out by search and rescue dogs today after terrorist attacks. In 2002 NYPD dog Apollo received the Dickin Medal on behalf of all the search and rescue dogs at Ground Zero and the Pentagon following 9/11. Their handlers described how: 'Faithful to words of command and undaunted by the task, the dogs' work and unstinting devotion to duty stand as a testament to those lost or injured.' An equally daunting task faced Labrador guide dogs, Salty and Roselle, on 9/11. Trapped in the twin towers they remained: 'loyally at the side of their blind owners, courageously leading them down more than seventy floors of the World Trade Center and to a place of safety.'

In 2001 the PDSA instituted a new medal, the Gold Medal. If the Dickin Medal was the Victoria Cross for animals, then the Gold Medal would be the animal equivalent of the George Cross – for civilians in peace time performing a heroic act, as opposed to those in the armed forces during war. All too soon there were candidates for the Gold Medal, as London experienced the terrorist bombs of 7 July 2005, and dogs stepped forward to do their best. Among the first to receive the Gold Medal was a British Transport Police explosives search dog, Vinnie. Vinnie and his handler, PC Dave Coleman, were already on duty in the City when they were urgently deployed to the terrorist explosion at Russell Square tube station. Vinnie immediately began a search

PC Dave Coleman and Vinnie © PDSA

for secondary explosive devices in order to establish a clear and safe route for medical assistance to reach the many casualties. Overcoming choking smoke and poor visibility, Vinnie then searched the mile-long route from Russell Square to the bomb-damaged train at King's Cross and completed a reoccupation search of King's Cross station.

Vinnie's medal citation comments: 'Despite the horrendous devastation and human trauma, Vinnie did not hesitate in carrying out his duties. His skills and tireless devotion to duty were instrumental in restoring public safety and he proved invaluable throughout this tragic event.'

While Vinnie was working in the Underground, over at Tavistock Square, police dog Jake and his handler, Police Sergeant Robert Crawford,

*Police Sgt Robert
Crawford and Jake*
© PDSA

rushed to help casualties who needed urgent attention after the bomb explosion on a double-decker bus. Jake immediately began a search of the street leading to the bus. Working through shattered glass and twisted metal, he secured a safe route for an explosives officer to investigate a suspect device on the bus and for paramedics to reach injured passengers. Jake also then secured an area close to the bus to enable a makeshift field hospital to treat casualties. With this achieved, the tireless Jake then moved on to help Vinnie with the aftermath of the earlier Russell Square bomb. His citation reads: 'Despite significant danger, Jake worked tirelessly and remained undaunted by the work presented to him. His skill, control and unstinting devotion to duty protected members of the public and the emergency services from harm.'

Police Sgt Robert
Crawford and Jake
© The Kennel Club
Friends for Life

"It's always 'Sit,' 'Stay,' 'Heel' – never 'Think,'
'Innovate,' 'Be yourself.'"

PC Rob Brydon-Brown and Billy © *PDSA*

Every emergency service was at full stretch as the horrifying events of 7/7 unfolded all over London, with the first bombing in the business district, the City. When City of London Police explosives search dog, Billy, got involved nobody knew what was happening. Billy and his handler, PC Rob Brydon-Brown, were called out to what was thought to be a train crash at Aldgate tube station. They arrived at a scene of devastation, with casualties everywhere, and from the nature of the injuries it was clear that there had been an explosion. Billy was tasked to secure the scene by searching the length of the underground tunnel. Despite immense heat and poor visibility, Billy remained constant to his duties and did not falter. He worked tirelessly, never letting the danger distract him from his determination to do his job. Billy's Gold Medal citation describes how he remained: 'On call throughout the day and attended twenty-one locations in response to alerts from the public.'

Both the PDSA Dickin Medal and the PDSA Gold Medal bear the inscription: 'For Gallantry.' Reading the stories behind the awards gives a very real meaning to the phrase. When the chips were down these dogs didn't waver for a second, selflessly stepping up to do whatever was asked – and more. It is good to know that organisations like PDSA are there to give help back to our brave best friends.

There are many ways of helping **PDSA** and its work for all animals. You can donate or give a legacy, or make a contribution to a particular appeal. If you want to get more closely involved you can become a PDSA volunteer or take part in a range of fundraising activities. There is even a PDSA on-line shop where you can buy a range of products. To find out more, visit the PDSA website at www.pdsa.org.uk or phone 0800 0199 155. If you prefer to write, the address is PDSA Head Office, Whitechapel Way, Priorslee, Telford, Shropshire TF2 9PQ.

CHAPTER SIX

STEP FORWARD
SUPER-DOGS!

The Kennel Club's Friends for Life Awards

CRUFTS IS THE WORLD's largest dog show – not a show for the world's largest dog, that is – but the single biggest gathering of nearly 28,000 dogs of every imaginable type, breed, personality and purpose there is. So you probably would find the world's largest dog there, along with the smallest, the prettiest, the most athletic, the cleverest, and, of course, the most heroic. Working dog competitions have been held at Crufts since it started in 1891. Over the years since then showing, agility, obedience and other classes have been introduced by the show's organisers, The Kennel Club. And in 2006 their Friends for Life award was launched, following on from the earlier 'hero dogs' title.

The Friends for Life award is made each year under the floodlights of Crufts main arena, just before the final competition for Best in Show. So the atmosphere is already electric before the six nominated 'super-dogs' step forward. The dogs aren't in the least bothered by the lights; the audience of more than 6,000 people; the p.a. commentary; the press – it's all in a day's work for a Friend for Life. Because these dogs, from all sorts

The Kennel Club's Friends for Life awards at Crufts dogshow © The Kennel Club Friends for Life

of backgrounds, have achieved feats that are beyond the normal experi-ence for any dog, and many humans. Some Friends for Life dogs work in the army, sniffing out explosives. Others are specially trained assistance dogs who make everyday life possible for their disabled owners. Not all the dogs are trained workers – many are just normal pct dogs or rescue dogs who have saved someone from drowning, or warned of a building on fire, or prevented their owner from stepping into traffic.

Nominations for the award can come from anyone, so there is huge variety in the dogs which eventually come forward. Unlike the born-in-the-purple showing dogs, these dogs come in every shape and size. Each is unique, with the dogs having an extraordinary range of talents: from the ability to sniff out cancer cells, to a talent for predicting if their owner

Assistance dog Josie with Sam Daly and mum Sara at the 2010 Friends for Life awards © *The Kennel Club Friends for Life*

is about to have a seizure. These dogs truly do have super-hero skills and it wouldn't be at all surprising to find one with x-ray vision or the ability to leap tall buildings!

For example, seven-year-old Rebecca Farrar's Labrador, Shirley, gives a constant accurate check on Rebecca's blood sugar levels, without the need for complicated blood-testing. Rebecca's aggressive type 1 diabetes was diagnosed when she was only four years old. Her mother, Claire, remembers it all too well: 'It was the May bank holiday weekend, and Rebecca had had some diluted blackcurrant juice, but she was thirsty and kept asking for drinks. Then she went to the bathroom and weed five times, and she was sick. We took her straight to the doctor's and he sent her to the hospital and she was admitted straight away. It was awful. Rebecca's twin brother Jason came to hospital with us and when they wanted to keep her in both of them were screaming down the corridor, and my mum had to drag Jason away. Rebecca was in hospital for four days. We had to keep giving her injections.'

Eventually Rebecca was stabilised, but the diabetes would be with her permanently, a disastrous situation for such a young child. Claire describes the stressful daily routine she and Rebecca were thrown into: 'I had to do blood-sugar tests on her five or six times a day – particularly when she had something to eat. Then she had to have an injection four times a day. If Rebecca wanted a little treat that would mean more tests and possibly another injection. The worst thing was that we would get no warnings if her levels were crashing.'

Shirley and Rebecca Farrar © The Kennel Club Friends for Life

Then Claire saw an advert in the local paper looking for social homes for Medical Detection dogs. Among other things, Medical Detection dogs are trained to alert for blood-sugar imbalances in diabetic people, so of course Claire was on the phone straight away: 'Rebecca was about five at the time. I explained about her type one diabetes and after being vetted, we went on the waiting list for about twelve months. It was a difficult time because Rebecca was getting imbalances; she kept collapsing and going into a deep sleep and we couldn't wake her up.

'Then the phone call came. Rebecca was six by then and we went to the Charity's office where we met Shirley. The Charity wanted to make sure that she would be suitable – but the pair of them got on really well together from the start. Then Shirley came for the weekend and stayed with us. It was very soon after that Shirley had her first alert. We were on holiday at Haven and Shirley did an alert – she got up from under the table and started licking Rebecca. I didn't really think there was anything wrong, but we did a test to be on the safe side and it turned out that Rebecca had gone down to 2.3 – which is very low, and we wouldn't have known without Shirley alerting us.

'Since then we have got used to the alerts. You can tell the difference between Shirley just being pleased to see you and an alert. When Rebecca is going imbalanced, Shirley licks her and licks her and won't leave her alone. Then Shirley gets the sugar testing kit for us. She's taught herself that – she realised that the first thing I always do is get the kit, so she goes and gets it herself!'

It's easy to understand how much Shirley has transformed life for the Farrars. Claire describes the day-to-day differences: 'Shirley comes everywhere, when we go shopping it is great because we can instantly treat Rebecca if her blood sugar is too low. Shirley will alert me, and a glass of coke or a Kit-Kat will bring Rebecca's levels back up. Sometimes they may have gone too high, and Shirley can tell me about that as well, so that I can test for an exact reading, and if necessary give Rebecca an injection to bring it down.'

One of the biggest breakthroughs is that Shirley is so well-behaved that she has become the first blood-sugar detection dog in the UK to be allowed into a main stream primary school. 'Shirley goes to school nine till twelve in the mornings,' explains Claire. 'She sits with her head on the desk and can alert the teachers, which makes it much easier for the teachers to cope. Before we had Shirley there was a problem one afternoon and Rebecca had gone really low and couldn't be woken. I was there within minutes, but had to phone 999 three times and I ended up driving her to casualty myself. Since we have had Shirley that's stopped happening, and I can even get some sleep because Shirley is alerting through the night. Rebecca is a more confident child when she is with Shirley.'

Rebecca agrees: 'Shirley is my best friend, she saves my life.' One of the best moments for Rebecca was when she and Shirley got nominated for their Friends for Life award. Everybody in the school voted for her and the family went to Crufts from their home in Northampton, and eventually won a crystal vase as runners-up. Claire says: 'It was brilliant, a great experience but nerve wracking! I was a bit concerned about Shirley because the hotel where we were staying was all white, and Shirley does like her playtime … There was a big lake where she was having her run, and I could see her heading that way and I was thinking of those white walls, but I got her to come back just in time!

'We have had Shirley for a year or so now and she is like two different dogs. You put the coat on her and she is working, she is good and really well behaved. Then, when you take her coat off she is hyper-active and chews and everything. She is only three years old, so she is very playful and she has to have free time. She can be naughty – she has been known to go into the teacher's handbag and steal her lunchtime sandwiches!

'Rebecca does the walking and the grooming and the brushing and gives Shirley a bath once a week so she is nice and clean for school. Rebecca has another three years at this school, and the next school she would have to get on a bus. We will have to take it one step at a time. But Shirley is part of the family now. She has given me and the school so much reassurance.'

So many of the owners of Friends for Life finalist dogs talk about their dogs having unique characters, and showing initiative far beyond what they have been trained to do. For the dogs to have their day at

Crufts is a wonderful chance to celebrate them as individuals. When the public sees assistance dogs going about their work, the image is often of a very serious dog that has no fun – we don't get a chance to see them let their fur down as their owners do!

For Tony Brown-Griffin, from Tunbridge Wells, this is an especially important aspect of life with super-dogs. She explains: 'You need a particular personality of dog. All four of my dogs have been different breeds – Collie, Golden Retriever, German Shepherd, Golden Retriever Labrador crossbred – and have been all very different. But they have certain personality traits in common – they have to be steady and completely bombproof. Cal, for example, was a seizure alert dog and he was a dog that was very stoic and took his responsibilities very seriously, however Rupert was fun loving and up for anything but also serious when working. Yet they enjoyed life, all the dogs have been very enthusiastic about their work. But adaptability is key. They have to have the ability to be in charge if necessary, and to cope with that. Particularly when alerting to seizures. Because I cannot hold a driving licence there is a lot of walking, so they have to have the energy. I visit Central London regularly and none of them have been bothered by crowds and different situations. Arthur, who's retired now, has flown all over the place with me – we went off to Texas together!'

As a trustee of the Support Dogs charity, assistance dogs are a big part of Tony's life – almost literally. About eighteen years ago Tony was a busy working wife, when she developed a severe form of epilepsy (she also has a degenerative eye condition which has resulted in her being registered blind five years ago). It was a difficult time for Tony, fighting illness and disability on several fronts, forced to take medical retirement, but trying to hold everything together despite her alarming and unpredictable epileptic seizures. She remembers: 'At that time I had Collies which I used to do obedience work with. My husband noticed that one of the dogs, Rupert, would occasionally behave strangely just before I had a seizure, so he wrote to an epilepsy society who told him about Support Dogs who were running a pilot study'.

At that time the charity had already trained its first seizure alert dog, so they knew that it was possible and decided to look more closely at Rupert: 'I went to get assessed, which seemed like a mad thing to do at the time, but soon enough Rupert became one of the first seizure alert dogs trained in the UK. He had been a rescue dog. He was very bossy and he was what I needed at the time. He bossed me around. He alerted me to a seizure and if I ignored him would tug at my trouser leg. He was always very persistent with his alerts. My short term memory is not very good, but he was the right kind of dog – very forthright! My current dog, Hetty, is a two-year-old Golden Retriever-cross, both a recognised guide dog and a seizure alert dog – the first to have done dual training in these fields. In addition to guiding me, Hetty warns me of an impending seizure. With a minor seizure she gives me fifteen minutes, and for a major, it is forty-two minutes, which usually enables me to get home. Wherever I am, it is the crucial time to help me get somewhere safe.'

A happy ending for Tony, but very far from the full story of the role of assistance dogs in the Brown-Griffin household. Just over eleven years ago, Tony's daughter, Grace was born. 'She was eventually diagnosed with autism and ADHD (Attention Deficit Hyperactivity Syndrome),' explains Tony, 'and to be honest it didn't come as that much of a surprise.' Grace's diagnosis means she has a learning disability, and a gluten intolerance which can lead to impulsive behaviour. With her knowledge of the often unlooked for ways in which assistance dogs can help, Tony began to wonder if having a dog could help Grace, particularly as Grace had a deep attachment to all animals, resulting in her being very much calmer when she was around them.

Support Dogs were doing a further pilot project for autism assistance, as they had previously had great success with a young child in Scotland. So Tony and Grace went through the application and Merlin was placed with Grace some months later. Tony explains: 'Merlin is a lively young Springer-Labrador cross, and he was on his fourth home by the time he was seven months old, when he was then donated to Support Dogs. He was a hooligan, but he was an honest dog through and through – mischievous but there was genuine niceness and solidness about him. My dogs liked him, and they can always tell.'

Tony didn't know what to expect, but immediately found big improvements in many different areas of Grace's life: 'Merlin sleeps in her bedroom at night, and because Grace used to try and leave the house in the middle of the night Merlin was trained to press a special alarm. Merlin would hit the alarm and then block the doorway – but one of the really interesting things was that Grace would stop to put Merlin's collar and jacket on. These days Grace has stopped trying to leave the house.

'It's impossible to work out if it is purely Merlin, but good things started happening when Merlin arrived. Before Merlin, Grace was very

Merlin and Grace Brown-Griffin © *The Kennel Club Friends for Life*

difficult to get to school. She wasn't reading and was writing very poorly. So Merlin would take her to school and wave good bye. Immediately Grace stopped struggling and screaming all the way to school. From being very, very distressing for all of us, one of her most difficult behaviours was curtailed.'

Merlin's positive impact on Grace has improved all her behaviours: 'He is a constant for her. If he is there, she knows everything is going to be all right which prevents her anxiety from building. He is very calm with her when she is having a bad time. She can be screaming and Merlin will provide comfort and that will stop her. It's particularly helpful on the social side that he wears his blue Support Dog jacket. One of the things we have noticed is that people would think Grace was just naughty and pass comment which would often escalate Grace's behaviour making things worse. Now with Merlin in his jacket, there is a much more positive social interaction as people can see that Grace has disabilities and is not a naughty child.

Friends for Life award nominees, left to right: Echo (with Mike Dewar); Merlin (with Grace Brown-Griffin); Kaiser (with Joanne Day); Shirley (with Rebecca Farrar); and Jake (with PSgt Robert Crawford) © *The Kennel Club Friends for Life*

107

'At her first school Grace was bullied but she talked it through with Merlin. It's a companionship she doesn't get from other children who don't understand her condition. And of course, having Merlin has given her a lot of street cred. Children who would not give her the time of day were interested in her. Merlin is a stepping stone, he can allow her to see that the things she used to be scared of are OK. I believe he is giving her a pathway through the autism, gradually showing her another way to cope.'

Merlin, Arthur, and Hetty with Grace, Miriam and Tony Brown-Griffin on a family adventure

The Brown-Griffin family is unusual in having two members with assistance dogs, but Tony feels it probably wouldn't be a family at all without them: 'I don't think my marriage would have survived all this without the dogs. I wouldn't have had my children without them. They are what makes it possible for us to have a proper family life – we are all off kayaking this summer.'

What a vision: canoe-loads of Brown-Griffins paddling off down the River Exe, complete with dogs!

Sadly Joanne Day, whose dog, Kaiser, won the 2011 Friends for Life award isn't able to do much physical activity, as she suffers from a rare condition called post-traumatic dystonia which leaves her limbs randomly fixed and contorted in extreme positions. Joanne received Kaiser, a Golden Retriever cross Poodle, from the Canine Partners charity in 2009. She vividly remembers the months leading up to that moment: 'Things had got very difficult. I had been studying for a Masters degree in Physiotherapy and unfortunately had to fight the university to remain in the course as a disabled student. They didn't think that you could be a student physiotherapist with a disability like mine. I had some surgery that went very wrong, leaving me in the position of having my leg bent up right in front of me. I managed to keep studying. But the pain was getting worse and it was hurtful that some people would even laugh about my leg, shouting 'Oh it's a flamingo woman!' Still, I did get my masters degree and qualified in June 2009.'

Eventually Joanne accepted that she needed some help, and Canine Partners found Kaiser for her. 'Kaiser has transformed my life in many ways. I rarely went out of the house before, but now I take him for his walk and everyone we meet along the way likes to stop and chat. He is so very cute and handsome that everyone just melts when they see him. I have met so many new people through taking Kaiser out, that I am now a lot more self confident. I used to have very little self belief but being able to continue the training with Kaiser and teach him new things has taught me to believe in myself again. People no longer laugh or point at me and the position of my leg, because they are transfixed by my dog.'

Kaiser and Joanne Day © *The Kennel Club Friends for Life*

Like all the Friends for Life partnerships, Joanne maintains that Kaiser has his own very independent status within the relationship: 'Kaiser is a big teddy bear and often acts like it. He loves his cuddles. When the trainers were around he was an A* assistance dog, but when they went, let's just say that he tested the boundaries with me. One day I said to my mum, 'He's so strong willed,' and she replied, 'That's what I have had to live with for thirty-six years.' Then it clicked, Kaiser is me in a dog!

'Kaiser has taught me that it's ok to let someone help you. Yes, I could still load the washing machine, but the pain and discomfort this causes is now saved by Kaiser doing it for me. It used to be that I wouldn't go out without having someone with me, just in case I dropped my purse, keys or phone as I so often did. Or even worse that, as I take my crutch off to get my purse out, it tumbles to the floor. Now I don't need someone there, because if this happens, Kaiser picks them up for me. And on top

Kaiser and Joanne Day
© *The Kennel Club Friends
for Life*

of that, he's my faithful best friend. I have had more than fifty operations and spent so much time in hospital that friends have just come and gone and I was becoming lonely. Kaiser is always there for me.'

Joanne also points out that as much as Kaiser is there for her, he is in some ways as dependent on her as she is on him: 'Whenever I may need him, he is there for me; working with Kaiser gives me a focus. It doesn't matter how I feel, Kaiser depends on me to get up, feed and walk him.

Kai, me and my crutches have been on walks where no crutches should ever be seen. I have crawled over gate posts and stiles just to ensure that he gets his thank-you walk. Before he entered my life, I was just getting through a day, and it seemed to me that my character had changed. Now though, Kaiser fills me with so much laughter and humour, and the number of stories I have about things he has done never seem to end.'

> **The Kennel Club Charitable Trust:** Many of the organisations training Friends for Life award winners have benefited from donations by the Kennel Club Charitable Trust, established in 1987 with the objective of making a difference for dogs. In the twenty-two years it has been operating the Trust has given over £4m in grants. In addition to its Charitable Trust, the Kennel Club runs a huge number of activities and programmes encouraging a positive relationship between people and their dogs, including the Young Kennel Club and the Kennel Club Good Citizen Dog training scheme. To find out more visit the Club's web-site at www.thekennelclub.org.uk

CHAPTER SEVEN

IN THE LINE OF DUTY

Dogs on Service in Britain's Armed Forces

D O DOGS KNOW WHEN they have done something heroic? Clearly they recognise that they are being praised and rewarded. This is how it is possible for we humans to train dogs – by giving positive reinforcement to the 'good' behaviours we want them to repeat. But throughout this book, another theme has emerged in the stories told by the owners of hero dogs. Most of the owners, even of dogs trained to perform 'heroic' tasks, report that the dog did what it did spontaneously, on its own initiative. Whether the hero dogs are simple pets, companions, assistance, or specific working dogs, everybody who has shared a special experience with their dog agrees that it was most definitely not performing 'a trick' or begging for a reward. The question I am repeatedly asked about my research into hero dogs is: 'Why did they do it?'

The immediate answer: 'Because they wanted to' isn't really an answer at all. It begs the question: 'Well, why did they want to?' In the case of military service dogs you might answer: because it's their job. And that's probably pretty close to the right answer. If you ask the

Sniffing a suspicious car in Iraq © *Wagtail UK*

question to a human hero – a soldier perhaps – who has just won the Victoria Cross, nine times out of ten, he or she will mumble modestly 'I was just doing my job.' Dogs and humans, just doing their jobs. Or rather doing their jobs as they perceive them to be. Most of us, faced with an oncoming tank or an unexploded bomb, would consider it our job to run, and run fast, in the opposite direction. But of course soldiers don't do that, and neither do their dogs.

Military dogs have appeared throughout this book, especially in the chapter on past winners of the PDSA's Dickin Medal for gallantry, but I don't think this is because they are more heroic than other dogs. It reflects that the nature of their work puts them in harm's way more frequently than other dogs. However, the trainers of service dogs – whether military or civilian, in the armed forces or the police – all agree that it does take a certain type of dog to cope with the demands of the job. They don't mean breed, although established 'working' breeds like German Shepherds, Labradors, Spaniels and Short-Haired Pointers are the most used. What they are really looking for is the dog's personality and temperament. Mike Dewar, Greater Manchester Fire Service dog

handler and trainer, says of his search Labrador, Echo: 'He is very head-strong and searches in his own way but he will always find. I trust him 100 per cent and I have come to respect his dominant side. That is his personality.'

Tony Brown-Griffin, a trustee of the Support Dogs Charity, says much the same of her dog Rupert, although his specialisation – alerting her to an oncoming epileptic seizure – was very different: 'Rupert was the first seizure alert dog trained in the UK. He had been a rescued dog. He was very bossy and he was what I needed at the time. He bossed me around.' As a professional trainer of service dogs, Collin Singer, managing director of Wagtail UK, defines very similar characteristics in the dogs his company provides for army and civilian work all over the world: 'The dogs are carefully selected for their drive. The gundogs are

A civilian sniffer dog helps the armed forces in Iraq © *Wagtail UK*

excellent, it has to be the type of dog that really wants it.' And PC Neil Mullett, dog handler and trainer with Kent Police, agrees: 'We need confident, assertive dogs with an outgoing, bold temperament.'

Interestingly, these character traits described by owners of hero dogs are very similar to those listed by recent research in the Harvard Business Review as the characteristics of good leaders among humans. The researchers described brave human leaders as having: 'High energy level and stress tolerance; self-confidence; internal locus of control; emotional stability and maturity; personal integrity; socialised power motivation; moderately high achievement orientation; and low need for affiliation.' Basically they are describing the kind of 'officer material' individual we all admire. Someone with bags of enthusiasm who is fairly unflappable, confident and level-headed and good tempered. This leader-type is certainly determined and has a will to win through, but without harming others in the process. They aren't prone to giving way to peer pressure – they are more likely to be setting a trend than following it – and most importantly they are positive people who do what they believe in. In other words, just the kind of person you can rely on in a tight spot. And oddly enough, in all the stories in this book, you can read those words being used to describe hero dogs by their owners.

These 'officer material' dogs would undoubtedly be pack leaders if they were living in the wild, and it may be that their courageous acts in coming to the aid of humans in distress spring from their natural urge to

Collin Singer of Wagtail UK training sniffer dogs for secondment to the armed forces © Wagtail UK

An MOD guard dog on patrol © *www.army.mod.uk*

protect the pack. Even though we are humans, the dog probably sees us as just another member of the pack and feels responsible! Military dogs, though, must learn to work side-by-side with their human handler – with the dog filling the role of sergeant to his human officer-in-command.

This was exactly the type of relationship Corporal Mike Mortimer, from the RAF Police Dog Squadron, had to develop with Bony, German Shepherd Force Protection dog, when on duty in Afghanistan recently.

Bony's job is to guard gates, fences and other vulnerable points at a camp, to make sure no one can make a surprise attack or plant explosive devices. It's a job you need to be tough to do, and Bony is tough. In fact, Cpl Mortimer told the *Sun* newspaper: 'Bony is hard as nails, and keeps you on your toes. He's always on the look out, always alert and doesn't seem to switch off. If you've got a weak handler and a strong dog, the dog will exploit you. But I'm getting him to chill out a bit.'

Military protection dog Bony © www.army.mod.uk

Dogs today play such an important role in the armed forces that they now have their own special regiment, the 1st Military Working Dog Regiment, which comprises the five different working dog units which have served in Bosnia, Kosovo, Northern Ireland, Iraq and Afghanistan. The new Regiment had its first formal parade in March 2010 under the command of Lt Colonel David Thorpe, who told the press: 'Military Working Dogs have been in the vanguard of recent and on-going operations in Iraq and Afghanistan and are key across the full spectrum of operations. The dog and its handler have a uniquely close relationship both in barracks and when deployed on operations. I have been immensely impressed by the dedication of all those involved and have witnessed the huge amount of time, personal effort, support and resources it takes to deliver a trained dog team onto the ground in Afghanistan. The formation of the Regiment is a further step forward in generating, optimising and sustaining Military Working Dog capability.'

The Regiment has 284 soldiers and officers and about 200 military working dogs, with home bases in the UK and Germany. At the moment its most important role is to support the dog units which are playing a vital part in Afghanistan – and as such it's welcomed by those out there. Major General Bruce Brealey, as the overall commander, commented at the launch of the Regiment: 'The formation of 1st Military Working Dog Regiment is making a major contribution to operational success every day in Afghanistan.'

A military police sniffer dog checks out the camera © *www.army.mod.uk*

A search Springer takes time out at Camp Bastion, Afghanistan
© *www.army.mod.uk*

The dogs have a number of roles in Afghanistan. Some, like Bony, are mainly guard and patrol dogs, helping with security at base camps and other key installations. Others will go out on patrol with the forces, searching and helping to clear routes, buildings and vehicles. Vitally important are the sniffer dogs, whose job is to search out explosives and mines. Private Kelly Wolstencroft, from Manchester, was one of the dog handlers on parade, with her Armed Explosive Search (AES) dog Molly. Kelly has been in the Army for three years. At the parade she told reporters: 'It is a real joy to work with these animals. It gives you great job satisfaction to know that you are working with dogs who are saving so many lives in theatre. And we also provide reassurance and a massive morale boost for the guys in the forward operating bases.'

One of the most famous of the Afghanistan sniffer dogs is Theo, a Springer Spaniel-cross, who has been nominated for a posthumous Dickin Medal. Theo and his handler, Lance Corporal Liam Tasker, were on patrol in Nahr-e-Saraj, Afghanistan, in March 2011 when L/Cpl Taskar was shot dead by the Taliban. Shortly afterwards Theo himself died of a seizure probably due to shock. Theo had already won praise for finding fourteen home-made bombs and weapons-hoards in just five months on the frontline – more than any other dog and handler in the conflict. When Liam was repatriated, a casket containing Theo's ashes returned home on the same aircraft. In a statement their commanding

Military sniffer dog the late Theo, with the late L/Cpl Liam Tasker
© P. A. www.army.mod.uk

On patrol in Afghanistan a US dog team is winched in
Photo US Army

The moment of truth for US army dog Rronnie
Photo by Spc. Aubree Rundle, US Army

In Afghanistan, US army dog handler Sgt Michael Hile prepares his partner 'Rronnie' to be hoisted by a helicopter Photo by Spc. Aubree Rundle, US Army

123

A military police sniffer dog in action
© www.army.mod.uk

officer, Major Caroline Emmett, said the team: 'had more operational finds than any individual team has had in Afghanistan to date and saved many lives as a result of this.'

So Theo is the latest recruit to the long list of hero dogs whose stories we will always tell.

For further information on military dogs, visit the army's website at www.army.mod.uk

APPENDIX

Charitable Organisations and How to Donate

Hearing Dogs for Deaf People – Trains dogs to alert deaf people and children. Website: www.hearingdogs.org.uk for news about the charity, plus details on puppy sponsorship, donations, fund-raising and legacies.

The Kennel Club – Involved in every aspect of life with dogs, including training and children's sections. Donates to other charities through its Charitable Trust, organises Crufts dog show.
Website: www.thekennelclub.org.uk for full details.

PDSA (People's Dispensary for Sick Animals) – Provides medical care for sick animals everywhere and makes the famous Dickin Medal and Gold Medal awards for animal bravery. Website: www.pdsa.org.uk for details of activities, shopping on-line, insurance, fund-raising and donations.

Support Dogs – Dedicated to improving the quality of life for people with epilepsy, physical disabilities and children with autism by training dogs to act as efficient and safe assistants. Website: www.support-dogs.org.uk for a full description and on-line giving.

Medical Detection Dogs – the umbrella organisation for Cancer + Bio-detection Dogs and Medical Alert Dogs, including diabetes dogs. Website: www.medicaldetectiondogs.org.uk for news from both charities and donations.

Dogs for the Disabled – Trains assistance dogs for children and adults with physical disabilities, and families with a child with autism. Through practical tasks our dogs offer freedom and independence, and give confidence to recipients. Website: www.dogsforthedisabled.org.uk for full information and donation details.

Canine Partners – A registered charity assisting people with disabilities to enjoy greater independence and a better quality of life, by providing specially trained assistance dogs. Website: www.caninepartners.co.uk for a full description of work, plus how to give.

Pets as Therapy – Provides therapeutic visits to hospitals, hospices, nursing and care homes, special needs schools and a variety of other venues by volunteers with their own friendly, temperament tested and vaccinated dogs and cats. Website: www.petsatherapy.org.uk for details of how to join in and fundraise.

Dog AID – Provides specialised training for people with physical disabilities using their own pet dog, rather than pre-trained dogs. Website: www.dogaid.org.uk for the full story and how to donate.

Assistance Dogs UK – A coalition of assistance dog organisations that encourages the exchange of ideas and best practice amongst its members. Website: www.assistancedogs.org.uk for more information.

National Search and Rescue Dog Association (NSARDA) – The overall organisation for several different search and rescue dog groups covering both mountainous and lowground searches in all regions of the UK. Website: www.nsarda.org.uk has links to individual groups and details of how to get involved or make a donation.

Animals in War – The Animals in War trust administers the memorial in Park Lane. Website: www.animalsinwar.org.uk to find out more or donate.

INDEX